JOHN JACOBSON'S

Dictionary OF DANCE

The Ultimate Guide for the Choral Director

Written by JOHN JACOBSON

Publications Available

08740693	Book	$16.95
08740695	Book/Video Pak	$39.99

HAL•LEONARD®
CORPORATION
7777 W. BLUEMOUND RD. P.O. BOX 13819 MILWAUKEE, WI 53213

Visit Hal Leonard Online at
www.halleonard.com

INTRODUCTION

Over the course of the last number of years I have tried to include in many publications choreography and staging notes that would help teachers, choreographers, students and performers in their attempts to add movement to their musical performances. I have always tried to write these notes in words and phrases that would be easy to understand even to beginner directors and their casts. Some of these words and phrases have been used by dancers and choreographers for generations and are quite universal. Others I simply made up as need be. Other choreographers will have different names for the same moves I have included here which certainly are as legitimate as any of these.

This book lists several hundred of the dance moves I use frequently and that you may see in publications I have had a hand in. I hope the definitions and pictures, as well as the video guide, will be helpful to you in your attempts to decipher my notes and adapt the suggestions to suit your individual needs. Some of these definitions will seem odd, some hilarious, some maybe even ridiculous. There is often no explaining the mind of a choreographer!

Naturally, there are unlimited possibilities as to how these moves can be interpreted, varied and executed. I invite and encourage you to do exactly that. I hope you will find these notes helpful. I look forward to an ever-expanding list as we all create the newest trends, and reprise the traditional, in the years to come.

John Jacobson

ABOUT THE AUTHOR

John Jacobson has choreographed, directed and performed in hundreds of staged productions throughout the nation and the world, including Grand Opening Ceremonies for Tokyo Disneyland in Japan, portions of the Macy's Thanksgiving Day Parade, and as choreographer for Ronald Reagan's Inauguration and The Singing Sergeants.

John received his Bachelor's Degree in Choral Music Education from the University of Wisconsin-Madison, where he performed in and eventually directed The Wisconsin Singers. He now holds a Master's Degree in Liberal Arts from Georgetown University. He has served as guest clinician at many national events, including Show Choir Camps of America, the Brightleaf Music Festival, and countless festivals, workshops, music education conferences, and reading sessions throughout the country. The highly successful John Jacobson Workshops are one-day choreography workshops first offered in 1988 under sponsorship of Hal Leonard Corporation.

John has worked as a consulting writer, choreographer, director and performer for Walt Disney Productions, while conducting seminars for students and music educators on a free-lance basis. He is creator and founder of the non-profit organization AMERICA SINGS! and has authored a video series as well as serving as co-author on a number of published choral revues and musicals, all available through Hal Leonard Corporation.

ABOUT THE BOOK / VIDEO . . .

Dictionary of Dance features 475 dance steps that have been compiled and presented in dictionary format for your quick reference! The steps are numbered and alphabetized by movement name, with cross references of related steps. Each movement is explained in the printed definition that follows, as well as demonstrated on the video. Several pictures and diagrams are also included in the book for further visual reference.

The dance steps are demonstrated on the video in the same order as listed in the book, with each step numbered and labeled. Please note there are a few steps in the book that are not included on the video.

1. 1ST POSITION — Standing with your legs together, heels touching, toes apart. A "parallel first" would mean that the heels and toes are together.

2. 1ST TIME — The first time through a section of music. For instance, if there are two verses, the 1ST TIME you would do the moves indicated along this line. 2ND TIME would refer to the second verse, sometimes indicated as "1X" and "2X."

A

3. ACCENT EACH DOWNBEAT WITH A THRUST OF THE FIST (90 DEGREES) — Swing your fist across the front of your body like a cheerleader saying "rah," or punch fist in the air.

4. ACCEPT DANCE POSITION — If an individual holds up their hands to another as if to ask "would you like to dance?", this would be the action of a partner taking those hands and stepping into position as if to accept the invitation.

5. ADD ON — This indicates a series of moves started by one person or group of people who are then gradually joined by another and then another and so on. The cast is adding onto the rest of the cast as they start to execute that move. This is an effective way of building intensity, much like a musical crescendo achieved by starting with one or more voices and gradually adding more and more.

6. AIR GUITAR — Pretending to play the guitar without actually having one in your hands. This is a very humorous move particularly in Rock and Roll, or heavy metal parodies.

7. AL JOLSON SHIMMY JAZZ HANDS AND KNEEL — The famous performer made this pose famous as he crossed the footlights, dropped to one knee, spread his shimmying fingers at ear level and sang, "Mammy."

AL JOLSON SHIMMY
JAZZ HANDS AND KNEEL

8. ALLIGATOR ARMS — Hold your arms straight out in front of you with one hand on top of the other, palms facing one another. Then open and shut those arms like the jaws of a big alligator. This is also referred to as "The Crocodile Smile."

ALLIGATOR: see also *411. The Alligator*

9. ALTERNATING TOE TOUCHERS — This is a move taken from physical calisthenics. The exerciser stands with feet apart and with arms outstretched at shoulder level. You bend at your waist so that your right hand reaches to touch your left foot. Then stand upright, and bend at the waist so that your left hand touches your right foot. This can easily be modified to make a very physical dance step.

10. ARCH JAZZ HAND — Open your hand with palm out to the audience and arch it overhead from one side to the other like a big rainbow from either direction.

11. ARCH RIGHT HAND OVERHEAD FROM L TO R — Move your right hand from left to right like a big rainbow. More specific instructions might include palm up, jazz hand, fist, etc. Variations would include "arch left hand overhead from R to L." This would be a good move to enhance words like *sky, fly, stars, clouds, everything, heaven,* etc.

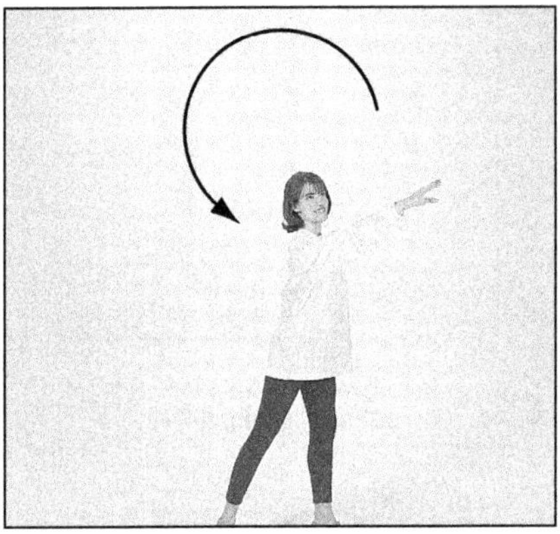

ARCH RIGHT HAND OVERHEAD

12. ARMS AKIMBO — Stand with your fists on your hips, elbows straight out to your side. This is generally seen as a very strong and confident posture.

13. ARMS CHEST OUT — A two-part move where you put your hands to your chest, usually with palms up and fingers together, and then reach both hands out toward the audience, as if to say, "I give this to you." This could also be performed with only one arm and any variety of hand positions.

14. ARMS OVERHEAD TOE HEEL TOE HEEL — Put your hands over your head in a snapping position. One foot at a time, crank your foot from toe to heel several times in a row. This could be used in both a 1950s Rock and Roll style, as in an Elvis Presley song, or in a character dance reflective of the peasant dances of Eastern Europe. It is appropriate for both men and women. For an interesting pattern, try 8 full counts on each foot, then 4 on each and finally 2 on each foot twice for a total of 32 counts.

ARMS OVERHEAD TOE HEEL TOE HEEL

15. ARM UP TO SHOW OFF BICEPS — Lift your 90-degree bent arm up so the upper arm is parallel to the floor at shoulder height and the fist is toward the ceiling. Flex your arm to show off your biceps.

16. ARSENIO PUNCHES — An arm gesture made famous by the talk show host Arsenio Hall. Raise arm overhead and punch the air in a circular fashion. It is used as a motion to encourage another performer or your audience to "GO! GO! GO!"

17. ATTITUDE — When talking about dance position, ATTITUDE refers to how the dancer is holding their legs. For instance, a BACK ATTITUDE (in a lift) indicates both legs are bent and held up to one side behind the dancer's waist. Usually the lower portion of the leg is behind the upper.

18. ATTITUDE HIP LIFT — One dancer is being lifted by another. The lifted dancer is holding their legs in a back attitude position. This is a beautiful lift when performed as the lifter turns in place, but can also be a dramatic position even when stationary.

ATTITUDE HIP LIFT

AXLE: see *135. Funky Skate Step - Axle*

B

19. BABY CARRIAGE LIFT — The lifter holds the lifted dancer around the waist and under the knees. The lifted person can hold the lifter around the back of the neck with one or both hands.

BABY CARRIAGE LIFT

20. BACK STEP (BS) — First, step back on one foot and then forward on the other, with a weight change as you move from one foot to the other.

21. BACKSTAGE — The area of the theater that is not in the audience's view. It includes the wings of the stage as well as the technical support areas, dressing areas, etc.

22. BACKSTROKE — A dance move that resembles the arm movements used by swimmers performing the backstroke. It was popular in the 1960s as a dance move. Simply rotate your straight arms in reverse direction from the shoulder.

23. BALL CHANGE (BC) — Step on the ball of one foot and then **shift your weight** to the other foot. While similar to a backstep, this movement is usually associated with an **uneven** rhythm where the step on the ball of one foot is shorter than the whole of the other. The "ball" might be an eighth note and the "change" a quarter note.

24. BALLROOM DANCE POSITION — Standing and holding a partner in a traditional dance pose. Facing each other, the male places his right hand on the female's lower back and holds her right hand in his left. The female's left hand is placed on the back of his right shoulder. This position would be commonly used in such dances as the Waltz, Polka, Foxtrot, Tango, etc.

BALLROOM DANCE POSITION

25. BASIC SOFT SHOE — This most common sequence of steps used in the soft shoe is made up of a series of steps and ball changes. Facing front, the dancer steps left on the left foot followed by a ball change (right/left) with the "ball" being downstage left of the left foot. This is on beats 1 and 2. On beats 3 and 4, this same rhythmic step ball change is performed beginning with the right foot with the ball change consisting of a left/right combination toward downstage right. Beats 5-and-6-and-7-and-8 are made up of a step to the left with three ball changes: (1) right left downstage left, (2) right left upstage right, (3) right left downstage left. Usually this 8-beat pattern would then be mirrored beginning on the right foot downstage right.

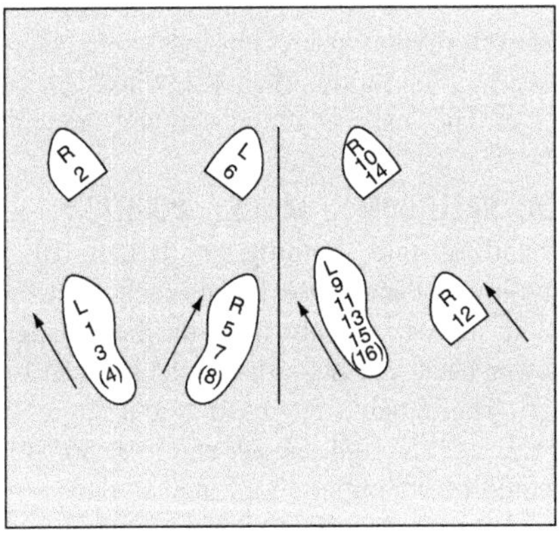

BASIC SOFT SHOE

26. BASIC SOFT SHOE 337 — Same as the Basic Soft Shoe. See above.

27. BEG — Clasp your hands as though you are begging, as if to ask "please?"

28. BEG HANDS — See "beg."

29. BELL ARMS (HELD HANDS) — As the cast holds hands, they swing them like the clangor of a bell. A common pattern would be to swing the hands 1/4 of the way to overhead and then back down to your sides. Then swing your hands 1/2 way to overhead and down. Next 3/4 of the way to overhead and down, and finally all the way to overhead. Like children swinging their held hands, this can be a joyful or dignified effort.

BELL ARMS

30. BELL KICKS — A kick to the side in which the heels come together in mid air with knees turned out. The kick is accomplished by stepping across the front with, for example, the left foot on beat 1, then lifting the right leg out to the right and bringing the left heel up to meet it on the next beat. This is then repeated to the other side to give the kicks a bell-like motion of swinging from side to side. It is a very popular and athletic maneuver used in country western dance, as well as sea chanteys, and many other character dances.

BELL KICKS

31. BIG KICK CHARLESTON STYLE (TOUCH FLOOR) — Step forward with your left foot and then kick the right foot as high as you can straight out to the front. The arms swing high overhead so the dancer looks like a place kicker on a football team. This is followed by a step back on the kicked leg (R in this case) for beat 3. On beat 4, you touch the floor with the left foot as far back as possible, while touching the floor with your left hand as well. It was very popular in a Charleston dance representing the 1920s. It can be performed with either leg.

BIG KICK CHARLESTON STYLE

32. BLADE HANDS — Holding your hands with fingers outstretched but together so they resemble the blade of a spear or knife. They can be with palms up, down or sideways.

BLADE HANDS

33. BOTH HANDS WAVE OVERHEAD — This usually indicates a move in which both outstretched arms wave together from the elbow left and right one time on each beat or even half of a beat. Great for high energy numbers such as certain Vaudeville style songs, or if performed more fluidly, the hands could resemble swaying palm trees.

34. BOW — This is the move performed in acknowledgement of the audience's applause. There are many variations of the bow from the formal GRAND BOW in which the performer bends deeply from the waist with his or her head being led by the chin, and the QUICK AND PERKY BOW in which the performer rises up on their toes at the beginning and end of the bow to give it an extra degree of youth and energy, to the simple dignified NOD OF THE HEAD. Bows are almost always performed with feet absolutely together.

BOW: see also *98. Eight Count Bow* and *143. Grand Bow*

35. BOW AND ARROW — This is an arm gesture that resembles the pulling back of an arrow before it is released from the bow. With fists together and stretched out at shoulder height to the left, pull the right fist with thumb extended to the right shoulder. A popular way to use this move is to simultaneously cross your right foot over your left as you "draw" the bow. Follow the move with a quick turn to the left pulling both fists to your waist as you turn.

BOW AND ARROW

36. BOWLING PIN FORMATION — A formation of multiple performers on stage that resembles the set-up of bowling pins. There would be one performer downstage in the first row. The next row would have only two performers slightly back and on either side of the front row performer. Each row back would simply add one more dancer until a bowling pin formation of any size is accomplished. This formation need not always be formed directly toward the audience but could be slanted, reversed, expanded or tightened up for a variety of looks.

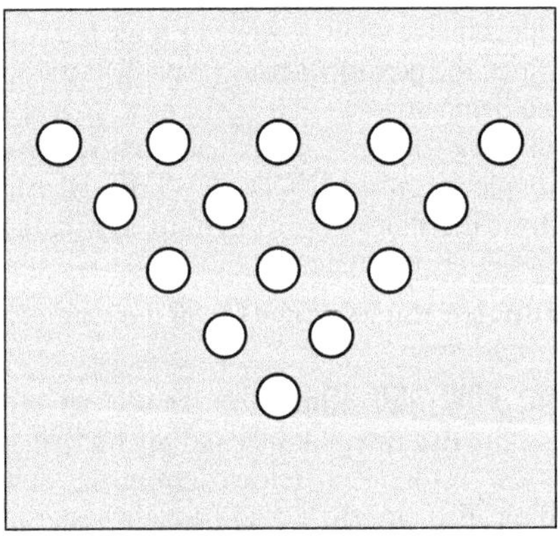

BOWLING PIN FORMATION

37. BOX STEP — The BOX STEP is one of the more common patterns of walking steps used by song and dance artists. It consists of four steps. Step One has the left foot stepping directly downstage. Step Two brings the right foot across the left. Step Three is a step with the left foot upstage of the crossed right. Step Four brings the right foot back to where it began to the right of the left. This can be started on any one of the steps as long as the pattern is continued for at least four steps. It can easily begin on the right foot and reversed so that the left foot does the crossover on beat 2. With minor variations, the BOX STEP can be used in almost any style of dance. If the knees are turned out it begins to look rather country in style. If a deep plié is used, it takes on a strong jazz flavor. With knees picked up high on each step, it can add to a Charleston or Ragtime routine. The BOX STEP is also often called a JAZZ SQUARE. The two terms are interchangeable, but BOX STEP is probably more common because it indicates a more versatile maneuver.

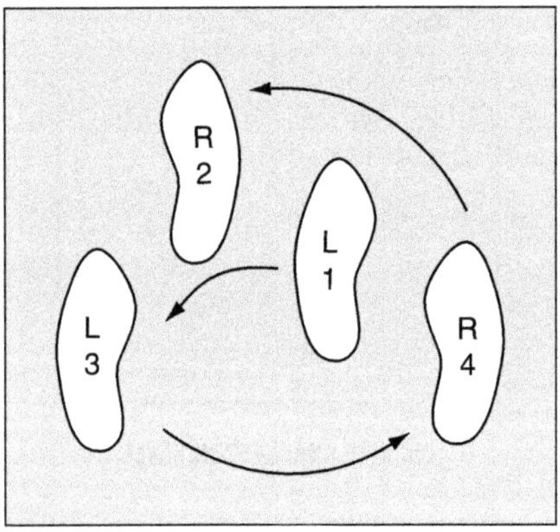

BOX STEP

BOX STEP: see also *73. Country Box Step, 93. Double Box Steps* and *94. Double Box Steps-Big Arms Pushing Straight Up*

38. "BRAVO" HANDS — Clasped hands, usually slightly above shoulder height, as in a gesture of "bravado."

39. BREASTSTROKE — Arm movements that resemble those of a swimmer when she does the breaststroke. The arms move from the chest outward toward the audience with the palms out as if to push the water out from in front of you. This dance was made most popular in the 1960s and 1970s.

40. BRUSH — A dance term used mostly in tap and soft shoe, a BRUSH is a sweep of the ball of the foot making it scuff across the floor and away. There is no weight change on a BRUSH as there would be on a FLAP. In other words, the total weight of the foot is not put onto the foot that is doing the brushing.

41. BUCKET OF WORMS — An undulating arm movement that consists of waving the arms in a developing swing out to the sides and slightly behind the dancer's body. The dancer leads the arm movement with the elbow and then gradually extends the lower arm and hand. This is usually done one arm at a time and can be accompanied with a step touch in the same direction as the arm that is being waved. If the group of dancers bend way over at the waist and raise each arm high and to the side as they develop the waving arms, it can resemble a can or "bucket" of slithering worms, with a little imagination on the part of the viewer!

BUCKET OF WORMS

42. BUFFALO BILL BOW — A flamboyant bow named for the famous showman of the old west. The performer plants one foot forward, removes his hat with a flourish and bows low, sweeping his hat across his waist. He then stands tall and uses his hat to present the American Flag, whether it is there or not.

43. BURST ARMS HIGH TO LOW — This is the action of bringing one's arms from overhead down to your sides. It can, but does not have to be, preceded by a clasping of the fists in preparation for bursting jazz hands that lower out to the sides. This can be done with a variety of hand positions from open jazz hands and palms up, to palms down.

BURST ARMS HIGH TO LOW

44. BURST ARMS LOW TO HIGH — The opposite of the above. This means bringing your hands and arms from below the waist to overhead in a sweeping motion, usually out to the side. It often is preceded by fists and then uses jazz hands or scooping palms.

45. BURST BOTH HANDS HIGH TO LOW (PALMS UP) — See BURST HIGH TO LOW. This is a more specific direction that instructs the dancer to specifically burst the hand from high to low with palms toward the sky as opposed to jazz hands or palms down.

46. BURST CLAP — First the dancer reaches both hands outstretched and overhead, with jazz hands most often. (This would not have to be a full extension of the arms, but that seems most appropriate to the situation.) Following this burst of outstretched hands, the dancer claps either overhead or at chest level.

47. BURST DOWNSTAGE HAND IN ARCH OVERHEAD — The hand that is closest to the audience bursts overhead from the opposite shoulder and forward. This might be called a "rainbow" arm in that the high arch would resemble the arch of a rainbow. This is a move that might indicate the sky, the sun, heaven or any other such lyric of height.

48. BURST HIGH TO LOW — See BURST BOTH HANDS HIGH TO LOW. This shorter instruction might be used in reference to one hand and arm, but is still a motion of the arm from overhead to lower.

49. BURST LOW TO HIGH — Again this might mean one or both arms but in any case would indicate that the dancer should raise that arm to overhead from a lower position usually preceded by a fist that opens to jazz hand as the arm raises.

50. BURST R HAND FROM EAR DOWN — This would more specifically instruct the dancer to arch the right hand from a position near the ear, in an arch moving away from the right ear. Of course, the same instruction could be given to the left arm and the left ear. The hand has probably been at the ear in a cupped position as if the dancer is listening to something.

BURST R HAND FROM EAR DOWN

C

51. CANES PARALLEL — When dancing with a cane, this instructs the dancer to hold the cane parallel to the stage floor unless more specific directions were included. There may be additional instructions as to whether or not the cane should be held with one or both hands and at what level, i.e. chest, waist, or overhead.

52. CARRIAGE — This word would be used in a couple of situations. In specific character pieces, it might be telling the dancers to assume a position as if they were riding in an old fashioned carriage or buggy. The girl could link her male partner's elbow with hers as he pretends to hold the reins of a pair of horses. There is also such a thing as a CARRIAGE LIFT, or more specifically a BABY CARRIAGE LIFT. This is accomplished by one dancer lifting another with one arm under their legs and the other under their waist. The lifted dancer usually would hold onto the lifter's neck or shoulders with one or both arms.

CARTWHEEL: see *258. Partner Cartwheel*

53. CENTERSTAGE — The middle of the staging area; technically a line running from the front to the back, or downstage to upstage, dividing the stage into equal parts. More specific directions usually would include "downstage center," "upstage center," or "midcenter stage," suggesting the proximity to the audience and the more specific spot on the stage.

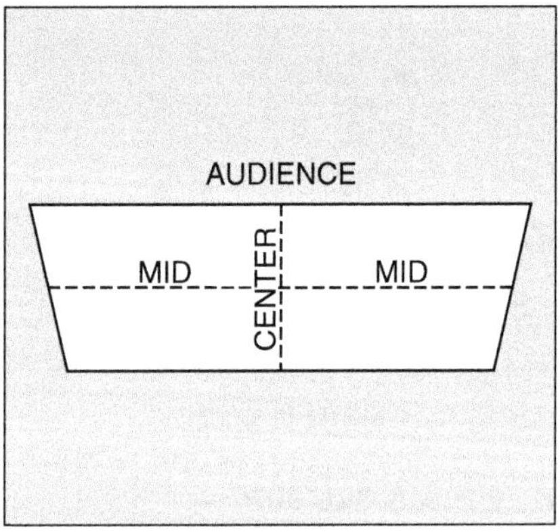

CENTERSTAGE

54. CHA-CHA — A fast rhythmic ballroom dance of Latin-American origin with a basic pattern of three steps and a shuffle.

55. CHAMPION HANDS — Like "bravo" hands, these are clasped hands at about shoulder level to either side. A sign of bravado.

56. CHAÎNE TURN — A French term for a full turn that uses three steps to rotate in one direction. Similar to a THREE-POINT TURN (see 419).

57. CHARLESTON — A lively ballroom dance of the 1920s in which the knees are twisted in and out and the heels are swung sharply outward on each step. The basic Charleston consists of one step touch to the front and one to the back with the palms of the hands showing to the audience and swinging from left to right and back.

CHARLESTON: see also *31. Big Kick Charleston Style (Touch Floor), 171. Hit Heel ala Charleston, 240. Men Pull Girls Through Legs ala Charleston* and *259. Partner Charleston*

58. CHARLESTON HANDS — Jazz hands held palms out toward the audience at about chest level and swung from left to right and back in a rapid and lively fashion representing the Charleston dance of the 1920s.

CHARLESTON HANDS

59. CHASSÉ — A French term for a dance step that consists of three steps in a dotted quarter note-eighth-quarter rhythm. The pattern is used to slide or glide across the floor.

60. CHEEK-TO-CHEEK IN DANCE POSITION — Couples standing in a traditional ballroom dance position with their respective facial cheeks pressed together for a romantic look as they dance.

61. CHORUS LINE — A formation of dancers standing in a long line as if being looked over by a panel of judges in an audition. There is a famous dance routine that begins the Broadway show, *A Chorus Line* in which the dancers step forward with their feet apart (LR) as they lift their jazz hands overhead also LR. Then they step back and bring their feet together LR as the hands come down (LR).

62. CHUGS — A dance step borrowed from the Charleston of the 1920s. The dancer jumps with both feet to one side and then to the other. You jump into the floor and bring your jazz hands from your thighs up to your chest level with each jump. This can also be performed in dance position with a partner.

CHUGS

63. CIRCLE RAINBOW ARM 360 DEGREES — One fully extended arm rotates from the shoulder to resemble the arch of a rainbow. It is a good move to indicate *sky, heaven, tree tops, etc.*

64. CIRCLE RIGHT ARM (RAINBOW ARM) — See CIRCLE RAINBOW ARM above. This is just a more specific direction.

C

65. CLAP (X) — The "X" in or above the musical score indicates where the dancer should clap.

66. CLAP BURST — A clap followed by a burst of hands usually in a "jazz" position. Like fireworks, the jazz hands slowly drop to the sides after the energetic percussion of the clap.

67. CLAP LOW AND IN FRONT — Clap directly in front of yourself, lower than your waist.

68. CLAP OVERHEAD — Clap directly overhead.

69. not on video

69. CLAP PRESENT HIGH — A clap at chest level followed by extended jazz hands straight up in the air. This is a very easy and exciting gesture when done in succession.

70. CLOG — A dance that was originally performed by dancers wearing clogs on their feet to beat out the rhythm on the floor. The clog dance is still performed widely but mostly with country and/or western music. Follow this 8-count pattern: step ball change, step ball change, step, step, step ball change (1 and 2, 3 and 4, 5, 6, 7 and 8).

CLOG: see also *234. March Clog*

71. CALLIOPE — In this instance the calliope would suggest that some members of the cast plié while others relevé, and then alternate between the two so that the movement of the cast resembles the up and down motion of the pipes on a calliope.

CALLIOPE

72. CONDUCT A FOUR PATTERN — Like the arm gestures of a conductor beating a four pattern, the motion is completed at head and chest level directly in front. The pattern is basically (1) both hands move down toward the floor, (2) hands move towards one another and may even cross slightly at chest level, (3) hands split apart toward opposite walls, (4) hands move toward the ceiling.

73. COUNTRY BOX STEP — *See 37. BOX STEP.* A COUNTRY BOX STEP uses the same four-step pattern that a regular BOX STEP does but includes some of the physical characteristics that make it look uniquely "countrified." This would include flexed feet, knees and toes "turned out," hands in a fist position or slapping your thighs on the offbeats, elbows prominent.

74. COUNTRY CRANK KICKS — "Fall" onto one foot as if you are going to run in the direction of that foot. On beat 2, crank the opposite leg out to the side with a kick at whatever height you deem appropriate. Then "fall" onto that kicked foot and repeat the crank kick step with the foot originally "fallen onto". This is used extensively in country/western or peasant dances.

COUNTRY CRANK KICKS

75. COUNTRY HEEL DRAGS — Step out to the left onto your left heel with the toes of that foot held up. At the same time, you lean into your left foot with your upper body so that your right hip juts out to the right. On beat 2, straighten up and bring your right foot toward your left so that the feet come together. (Step - drag, step - drag.) Hands are usually held behind the back, thumbs in front belt loops or holding a belt buckle, or fingers entwined with palms toward the floor.

COUNTRY HEEL DRAGS

76. COUNTRY STEP KICKS OUT TO THE SIDE, FLEXED FEET — Step across the front with your left foot and then kick your right foot directly out to the right side, keeping your right foot flexed and your shoulders square to the audience. Then step across the front with that right foot and kick a flexed left foot out to the left.

COUNTRY STEP KICKS OUT TO THE SIDE, FLEXED FEET

77. COUPLES BRING OUTSIDE HANDS TOGETHER BY HEARTS — An old fashioned pose by two people that indicates schmaltzy romance. The couples hold each others' hands in theirs, and lean toward each other with their clasped hands at about heart level. Usually the downstage foot is pointed away from the partner.

COUPLES BRING OUTSIDE HANDS TOGETHER BY HEARTS

78. COUPLES FACE EACH OTHER HOLDING BOTH HANDS AT CHEST LEVEL — See previous definition.

COUPLES: see also *183. Holding Both Hands, Turn Women Under so Couples Are Hugging Back to Front*

79. COUPLES HOLD UPSTAGE HANDS AND STEP SNAP APART, TOGETHER ETC. — Holding the hands that are away from the audience, the couple steps away from the partner on (1) and snaps the fingers of their free hand on (2). Then they step toward each other on (3) and snap their fingers at the direction of their partner on (4). The foot pattern is basically a "step touch" pattern.

COUPLES HOLD UPSTAGE HANDS AND STEP SNAP APART

80. COUPLES U-DIP HOLDING FRONT TO BACK — A couple stands facing the same direction with the male behind the female and holding her arms in his. The U-DIP consists of plié-ing (bending your knees) on beat 1 and straightening them on beat 2, while making a U-shaped motion with your entire body. *See 440. U-DIP.*

COUPLES U-DIP HOLDING FRONT TO BACK

81. COUPLES WALK UPSTAGE WITH BACKS TO AUDIENCE HOLDING HANDS — An action by a couple that has them walking away from the audience as though they are walking off into the sunset together.

82. COUPLES WALTZ IN CIRCLES AROUND THE STAGE — This would indicate there are several couples on stage that are waltzing not only around themselves but in a circular pattern that moves around the stage.

83. CRANK R ARM ELBOW FASTENED AT HIP — A Rock and Roll guitar player kind of move that has the dancer's right arm fastened to his or her hip at the elbow and circulating underhanded as if you were really strumming a guitar. Usually the left fist and arm would be extended out to the left side to simulate the neck of the guitar.

CRANK R ARM ELBOW FASTENED AT HIP

84. CRANK R LEG BEHIND WITH KNEES TOGETHER 1920s STYLE — A popular dance maneuver associated with the Charleston and other high energy dances of the 1920s where the dancer fastens their legs together with the right knee held tightly against the back of the left. The left leg stays firmly planted to the ground while the right lower leg does full 360-degree rotations, like a propeller, from behind.

CRANK R LEG BEHIND WITH KNEES TOGETHER 1920s STYLE

CRANK KICKS: see *74. Country Crank Kicks*

85. CROCODILE SMILE — A dance step made popular in the HOP 'TIL YOU DROP song collection. (See page 70.) The dancers extended their arms fully out in front of them at about mouth level. Palms are together with one hand on top of the other. Then the dancer opens and shuts these straight arms in time with the music like the jaws of a big crocodile.

86. CROSS ARMS OVER CHEST — With both hands in fists, cross your arms at the middle of your forearms and in front of your chest or face. It is a posture that can indicate *bondage, slavery, captivity,* etc.

87. CURTSY — A formal and feminine maneuver used to greet others or to acknowledge applause. The dancer places one foot behind the other and pliés at whatever level seems appropriate to the occasion. Generally, the deeper the curtsy the more formal the occasion. She may also dip her head at the same time she pliés, and may hold her skirt slightly out to the side.

88. CUTAWAYS — An athletic dance step associated with the Charleston, Drag, or energetic Broadway-style tap dancing. The dancer (1) jumps on both feet, then claps on the "and of 1," (2) jumps on to the left foot with the right foot coming up behind and getting ready to kick on the "and of 2," while at the same time the arms cross low and in front or overhead, and then extend out to the side on the kick, (3) the dancer repeats the step kick to the other side, and (4) repeat the first step kick. The arms have continued to scissor on each step kick.

CUTAWAYS

CUTAWAYS: see also *113. Feet-Less Cutaways* and *151. Half Cutaways*

D

89. DANCE POSITION "DIP" PARTNER — In a traditional ballroom dance position, the male partner rotates and dips the female so that she is close to parallel to the floor. This can be executed at any depth from the girl's hands slightly clasped behind the boy's neck, or to a much deeper drop with arms extended or maybe even held by one hand.

90. DEATH DROP — An extreme version of the partnered DIP in which partners hold each other's hands as the female is dipped almost to the floor. Both couples' arms are fully extended in a fully executed DEATH DROP.

D

DEATH DROP

DIVE: see *295. Pretend to Dive*

91. DO SI DO — Taken from country square dancing, the DO SI DO really means to just walk, skip or run around your partner. Usually this will be executed while circling yourself. In other words, there will be a time when the partners are front to front, side to side, back to back, side to side and then front to front again in one complete DO SI DO revolution.

92. DO SI DO SKIPPING — means to simply skip around your partner in a DO SI DO fashion.

93. DOUBLE BOX STEPS — A BOX STEP to each side separated by a ball change in order to switch feet. An example would be: (1) step forward L, (2) step across front R, (3) step back L, (4) step out to the right side R (and 5) ball change LR, (6) step across front with the left foot, (7) step back R, and (8) step to the L. All of this would be executed with shoulders basically square to the audience.

94. DOUBLE BOX STEPS - BIG ARMS PUSHING STRAIGHT UP — First see DOUBLE BOX STEP above to get the feet pattern. Both arms are fully extended toward the ceiling on each step and brought down to the shoulders on the "ands" of each beat. This is a very energetic dance appropriate for Charleston-type dances or country dance.

95. DOWNSTAGE — The area of the stage closer to the audience than any reference point. This can also mean a direction as in "move downstage" which would mean move toward the audience.

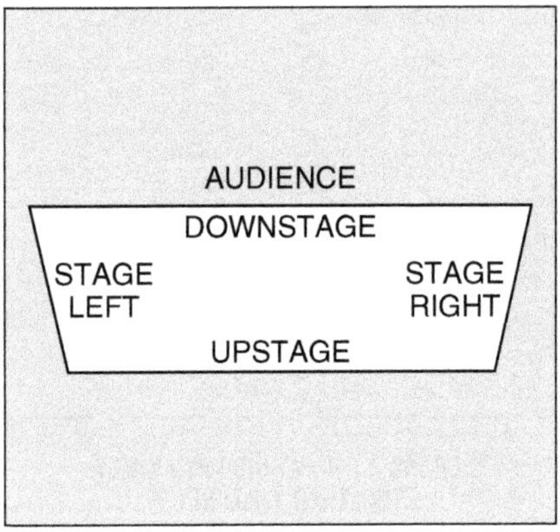

AREAS OF THE STAGE

96. DRAG BACK STEP — While facing the audience, (1) take a big step with your left foot toward stage left, (2) drag your right foot using a full two counts to do the drag, and follow this with a back step (RL) on beats (3) and (4). Repeat to the other side.

E

97. EDDIE CANTOR SKIP — Named after a famous performer. The dancer skips in place with knees turned out. You could also clap hands at the same time using only the fingertips of each hand and moving the hands in a circular pattern.

98. EIGHT COUNT BOW — A sign of acknowledgment that takes 8 full counts to execute. Feet are together throughout. (1-3) Stand up straight, (4) relevé, (5-6) bow low bending from the waist, (7) stand up straight and relevé again, (8) lower heels to stand on full feet. This entire move could be done twice as fast for a perkier bow.

99. EIGHT-COUNT TWIST — A 1950s and '60s twist pattern that uses an eight-count pattern to make it more uniform. Facing the audience the entire time with shoulders square to them, (1) twist at the waist and bring the right knee across the front and to the left as the upper body (especially arms) twists to the right, (2-3) lower that right knee and twist both knees right/left, (4) raise left leg across the front to the right as upper body twists left, (5-6) twist lower body left/right, (7) repeat the right leg across front as in beat 1, and (8) lower right leg. Repeat entire 8 counts starting once more with the right leg across.

100. ELASTIC ARMS — Any movement or extension of the arms that reflects a sense of tension so that there is strength to the move. The arms are like rubber bands being stretched in a certain direction only to be pulled back into place. Usually this move is used to reflect a certain musical motif that has that same elastic feel.

ELBOWS: see *120. Flap Elbows* and *227. Link Elbows*

101. EVEN FOUR-COUNT GRAPEVINE WITH HEEL ON FOUR — Four even walking steps with shoulders square to the audience. (1) The first step is directly out to the left side with the left foot. (2) The second step uses the right foot to step either behind or in front of the left still moving to the left. (3) The third step is another left foot step out to the left. (4) For the fourth step, dig the heel of the right foot out to the right in a touch. Repeat to the other side beginning with a step onto the right foot and out to the right.

F

102. FACE L REACH R HAND TO THE AUDIENCE — A direction such as this simply means to face stage left and reach your right hand toward the audience. It may on occasion give more specific directions such as palm up, point, feet together or apart, etc.

103. FACING DOWNSTAGE R ACCENT HIPS LRL RLR — A fun dance for either country or Rock and Roll. The hips accent left right left on beats 1 and 2, and right left right on beats 3 and 4.

104. FAMILY PORTRAIT — A grouping of dancers posed as if they are a family having their portrait taken or painted. Those in front must be low, and those in back are high so no one's face is hidden. An "OPEN" family portrait would suggest that the cast is not too close together, and "CLOSED" would indicate a tighter formation.

105. FEET APART, HANDS ON THIGHS BOUNCE — Stand like a baseball infielder waiting for a ground ball. Feet are at least shoulder width apart. Hands are resting on the front of your thighs.

106. FEET APART FACING FRONT, SWITCH WEIGHT FROM FOOT TO FOOT — Put all of the weight onto your right foot and extend your left out to the left side. The supporting leg is slightly bent. Shift your weight to the left foot as the left leg goes out to the side. Repeat this several times not letting your head go up and down as you switch weight.

FEET APART FACING FRONT, SWITCH WEIGHT FROM FOOT TO FOOT

107. FEET APART HANDS ON KNEES — Almost the same as FEET APART HANDS ON THIGHS, except that the hands are lower and resting on the knees as opposed to the thighs.

108. FEET APART ROCK SIDE TO SIDE SLAPPING THIGHS ON 1 AND 3 — With feet in a wide second position, shift your weight from left to right slapping your legs on the beat. This will be easy to execute with younger performers. However, for a more accurate "country" feel, continue the weight changes on beats 1 and 3, but slap your thighs on the offbeats of 2 and 4.

F

109. FEET APART SWING HIPS ("POOH" HIPS) — Named after everyone's favorite Winnie the Pooh, simply place your parallel feet far apart bending your knees slightly so that you "sit" into the position a bit. Now swing only your hips to and fro with jazz fists held at the side of respective hips.

110. FEET IN SECOND, BOUNCE 1,2,3, BRING THEM TOGETHER/APART ON "AND 4" — This is a routine borrowed from the "hip hop" moves of the 1990s. Again you are bent from the hips slightly, sitting into the position. Generally this routine is performed first with the switch happening on "and 4" of two successive measures. Then, the dancers continue the pattern but with the switch happening twice as often, such as on "and 2" and on "and 4." This would hold true for one complete measure. Finally, the performers quicken the step so the feet switch on the "and" of very count. The entire pattern is counted: "1,2,3 and 4, 5,6,7 and 8. 1 and 2, 3 and 4, and 1 and 2 and 3 and 4." This constitutes a total of 16 counts.

111. FEET IN SECOND, HANDS ON KNEES — Feet are apart, usually at about shoulder width or more. Hands are placed palms down either directly on the knees or slightly above them. This resembles the resting position of a baseball infielder.

112. not on video

112. FEET APART, HANDS ON THIGHS AND BOUNCE — Feet are apart, usually at about shoulder width or more. This is the same as the above definition except that the direction more specifically instructs the performer to place the hands above the knees and on the thighs.

113. FEET-LESS CUTAWAYS — This is a more controlled version of a full cutaway, designed to be used when the dance needs to be active but less athletic. The performer simple wipes one straight and fully extended arm over the other in a "scissoring" motion. This can be performed at any level in front of the dancer from below the waist to way overhead.

114. FIFTH POSITION — Taken from formal ballet and jazz dance terminology, this basically instructs the dancer to stand with feet together, "turned out," with one foot in front of the other. Usually the heel of the front foot is at about the ball of the foot that is behind.

FIRST POSITION: see 1. *1st POSITION*

FIRST TIME: see 2. *1st TIME*

115. FISHING POLE — This literally instructs the dancer to pretend to hold an imaginary fishing pole. It may or may not suggest that he or she also pretends to "reel in" on an imaginary fishing reel.

116. FIST IN THE AIR — Hold or punch your fist directly overhead.

117. FIST TO HEART PROUDLY — Hold your fist to your heart with the knuckles toward your chest in a posture of pride and/or patriotism.

118. FIST SHOULDER UP — Take one fist and in a two-count move, bring it first up to your shoulder and then overhead. This is a very powerful, almost cheerleader-like move.

119. FISTS ON HIPS — Sometimes described as standing "akimbo." Elbows are forward and the knuckles of the fists are placed on their respective hips.

120. FLAP ELBOWS — Using your elbows like the wings of a chicken, this action can have a ridiculous "Funky Chicken" look to it or, if performed higher up, can look decidedly Caribbean or Latin.

121. FLAPS — A FLAP means that you brush the toes of the foot on the floor as it moves away from your body and then immediately place weight on that same foot. The two parts of the move make a "fl—ap" sound.

FLAPS: see also *329. Running Flaps*

122. FLEXED FOOT — The opposite of "pointed foot." The toes of the foot are brought up as close to the same shin as is possible.

FLEXED FOOT

123. FLICK KICK — A two-count move that begins by stepping one direction as if you are going to run that way. Then you reverse direction and kick that same foot that you were stepping onto up and behind. That kicked foot will usually take on a "back attitude" position as it is kicked.

124. FLICK R HAND UP DOWN — A quick up-down gesture with the R hand in which you throw that hand high overhead, usually with the palm down and then bring it immediately to your side. It has a "woof boom!" sensation to it. Of course, it could be performed with the left (L) hand as well.

125. FLICK WRISTS PALMS DOWN LOW TO HIGH WITH BLADE HANDS — Fingers are held together, the palms of both hands are down. Beginning from low to high, the hands are flicked on each beat of the music as if there is something on the fingers you are trying to rid yourself of.

FLIM FLAM: see *342. Shim Sham (Flim Flam)*

126. FLIP FROM BABY CARRIAGE LIFT — Hold your partner in a BABY CARRIAGE LIFT (one arm under the back of the legs and one behind their waist.) Then toss the lifted partner's legs back and over their head so they perform a complete somersault landing with both feet on the floor. Make sure you are well spotted and supervised while rehearsing this move.

(Editor's Note: the "lift" video John refers to on the video is from "Step 2" of *Gotta Sing, Gotta Dance,* #08414585.)

FLIP FROM BABY CARRIAGE LIFT

FLIP: see also *241. Men Pull Women Over Back in a Full Flip*

127. FOCUS ON EXIT SIGN ABOVE AUDIENCE'S HEAD — This is a verbal instruction that will help performers unify their focus points. If all performers' eyes are focused on a real or imaginary "EXIT" sign at the back of the auditorium, the look can be one of vision, determination and unity. This is an excellent device to use with novice performers, but works equally well with performers of greater experience when you are attempting to focus the effort.

128. FOLD ARMS OVER CHEST — An impatient looking move, or one that indicates resolve. The performer stands with arms crossed over their own chest.

129. FOUR-COUNT GRAPEVINE AND HOP TOGETHER — This step actually uses five steps in four counts that completes a pattern and moves the performer stage left with shoulders square to the audience. (1) First step out L with the L foot. (2) Then with the R foot, step L either in front or behind the L foot. (3) Step again to the L with the L foot. (And 4) hop RL to bring the feet together.

F

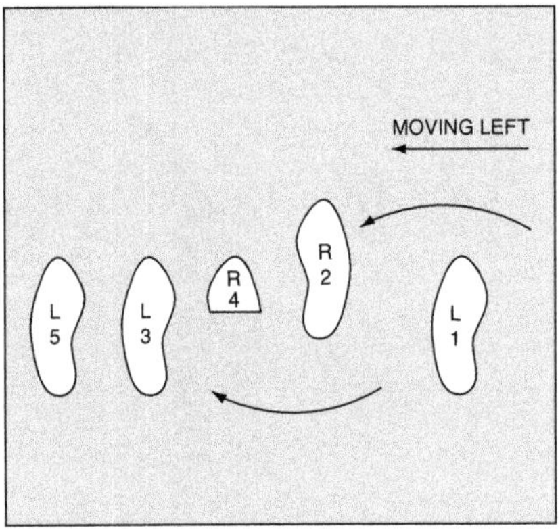

FOUR-COUNT GRAPEVINE AND HOP TOGETHER

130. FOUR GROUP PEEL OFF — A succession of the same move performed like dominos with four different groups usually placed in sequential order on the stage. For example: Group 1 claps their hands, followed by Groups 2, 3 and 4 in order for a rippling effect.

131. FOUR-POINT PIVOT — An 8-step move that involves two steps toward each wall with the performer making one complete turn around but not actually going any place. Each quarter turn happens as a pivot on one foot, for example the left, if you are actually turning to your left.

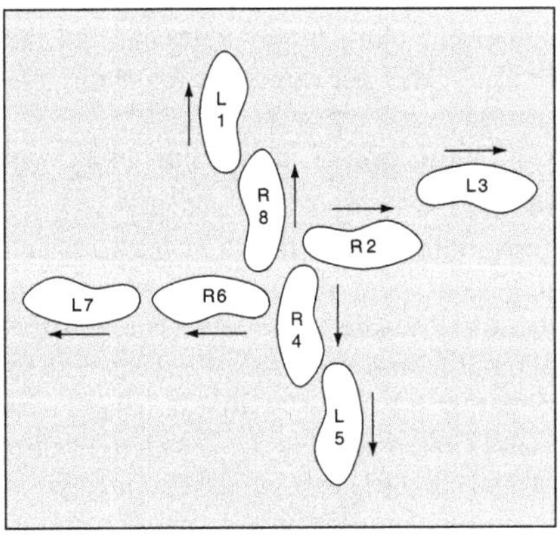

FOUR-POINT PIVOT

132. FRED ASTAIRE DRAG STEP — Named for one of the greatest show dancers of the American musical theater, this smooth and graceful move is reminiscent of the great Fred Astaire. Step to the left with shoulders square to the audience. This long step takes two full counts and has the arms extended in a diagonal pattern leading with the left arm up high and the right trailing low. On beats 3 and 4, the dancer performs an even back step (RL). Repeat to the other side leading with the R foot and the R arm high.

FRED ASTAIRE DRAG STEP

FREDDY: see *412. The Freddy*

133. FREESTYLE — This simply means "do your own thing!" However, it generally implies that "your own thing" will be appropriate to the music to which you dance.

134. FREEZE — Stop whatever you are doing in the position that you were doing it.

135. FUNKY SKATE STEP "AXLE" — Pretend to be skating first L, then R, then twice to the L. Repeat pattern to the other side, skating R L R R. The hands are usually complementing the move, stretching as if you are pulling a thread.

FUNKY SKATE STEP "AXLE"

OFFERED ELBOW

136. FUNKY CHICKEN — A ridiculous dance in which the performer flaps their elbows like the wings of a chicken and their knees like a cymbal-playing "one-man-band."

137. FUNKY STEP TOUCHES BEHIND — Step touch with the "touches" placed behind the "steps," often accompanied by elbows and fists that swing up on the "step" and cross in front and low on the "touch."

138. not on video

138. FUNKY STEP TOUCHES (HEEL) IN FRONT — Step touches in which the step is directly out to the side and the touch is actually in front of that step and uses only the heel of the touching foot.

G

139. GIRLS ACCEPT OFFERED ELBOW — The direction assumes that someone has offered the girl their elbow as if a walk arm-in-arm is being suggested. On the indicated beat of the music, the girl would link her arm into the offered arm, usually from behind.

140. GOSPEL STYLE STEP TOUCH — This step touch style is borrowed from the traditional Gospel style choir. It involves stepping one direction and then backing into that direction as you touch with the whole of the other foot. Then you repeat the move by backing into a step touch on the other side.

141. GRAB AIR WITH HAND — Grab a handful of air at about head level or a bit higher. It suggests that you are *catching something, seizing the moment or the day.*

GRAB AIR WITH HAND

G

142. GRAB THIGHS — Hold onto your thighs with your thumbs on the inside and the other four fingers of your hands on the outside.

143. GRAND BOW — An acknowledgement of your audience that is slow, full and dramatic. Bending from the waist, the bowing performer will often lift their chin to let their chest lead the bow and their head follows. The feet are together and legs remain straight throughout.

144. GRAPEVINE AWAY FROM AUDIENCE — Facing one side of the stage or the other, the performer executes a grapevine beginning with their upstage foot and moving away from their audience. For instance if you were facing stage L, you would begin the grapevine with your left foot and move to your left, upstage away from your audience.

145. GRAPEVINE DOTTED RHYTHM — This grapevine uses the same pattern of steps that any other grapevine uses but specifically calls for a dotted rhythm to be used in the stepping pattern. Usually that pattern will begin with an eighth note followed by a dotted quarter and alternate that pattern for as long as the grapevine lasts. It could however, begin with the longer valued note making the accent on a different portion of the beat. The difference is "and 1 and 2 and 3 and 4" as opposed to "1 and 2 and 3 and 4."

146. GRAPEVINE EVEN RHYTHMS — A grapevine performed with each step receiving equal value (for example, one quarter note per step whether it be the leading or the following foot.)

147. GRAPEVINE LONG — An eight-count pattern of marching in which the shoulders of the dancer are square to the audience throughout. The first step is directly out to the side, followed by a step behind or in front, still moving in the same direction. This is followed by six more steps of a similar nature alternating between steps behind and in front. This can be used in almost all styles of music with the real character of the routine added from the waist up.

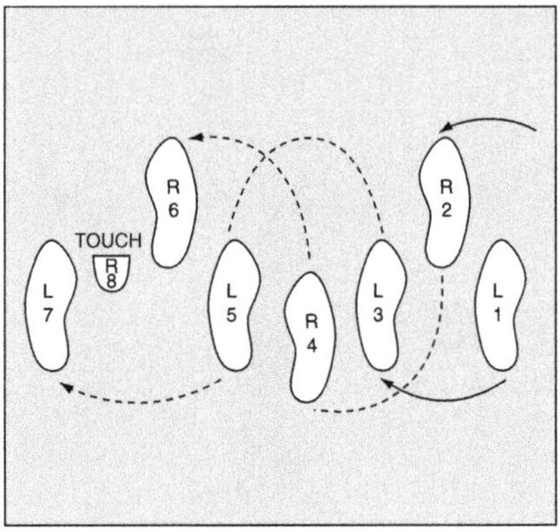

GRAPEVINE LONG

148. GRAPEVINE SHORT — A shorter version of the 8-count grapevine. The shoulders are held square to the audience. The first step is directly out to the side. The second step moves in the same direction as the first and crosses either in front or in back of the first. The third step is moving still in the same direction with the leading foot. Finally, the other foot simply touches out to the side with a toe, heel or full foot.

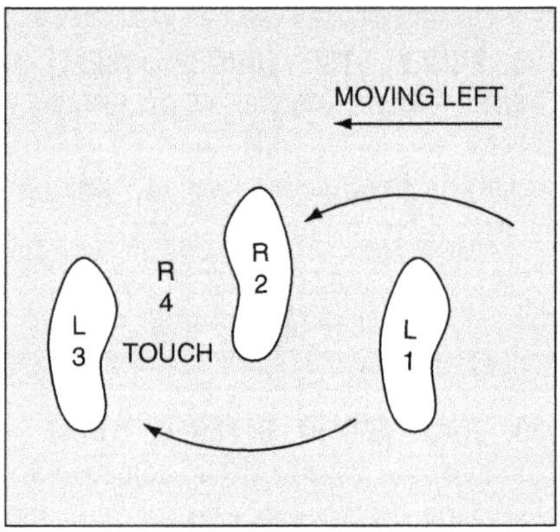

GRAPEVINE SHORT

GRAPEVINE: see also *101. Even Four-Count Grapevine With Heel on Four* and *129. Four-Count Grapevine and Hop Together*

149. GROUCHO MARX CIGAR GESTURE — Made famous by this great comedian, the performer pretends to flick the ashes from a big cigar and raise their eyebrows mischievously.

GROUCHO MARX CIGAR GESTURE

150. GUYS TAKE CENTER — This stage direction simply instructs the male dancers to assume a position stage center perhaps replacing another group of performers. The word "take" means assume or claim that territory.

H

151. HALF CUTAWAYS — Facing at an angle to one side of the stage, (for example, stage L) the weight is on the full R foot on each strong beat. The left foot will remain behind throughout the move and will briefly take the weight on the "and" of each beat. (This is essentially a "step ball change ball change ball change" pattern.) The palms are down, arms are open with the R hand slicing down on each step and the L arm high, overhead and behind at the same time. The hands will cross in front of the dancer at about chest level on each step of the left foot, (or the off beats).

HALF CUTAWAYS

152. HALF TIME MARCH — Marching one step for every two beats. Usually, the feet are both on the ground for the actual step (beats 1 and 3) with alternating knees coming up on the offbeats (2 and 4). The arms usually work with 90-degree elbows alternating to hold briefly at chest level on each step (1 and 3).

HALF TIME MARCH

153. HAND ala "TELEPHONE" — Hold your hand (in a partial fist) to the side of your face with the thumb pointed close to the ear and the little finger close to your mouth. The other three fingers are curled into a fist so that the hand resembles a telephone that you are pretending to speak into.

H

154. HAND INDICATES $$ — Hold your hand palm up and rub together the thumb with the next two fingers as if you are indicating money.

155. HAND JIVE — A 16-count clapping and slapping pattern made famous in the 1950s and '60s but well known even today.

1-2: Slap your thighs two times.

3-4: Clap twice.

5-6: Slice your right hand two times over your left in a scissoring move.

7-8: Slice your left hand over your right in a scissoring move.

9-10: Pound your right fist on top of your left two times.

11-12: Pound your left fist on top of your right two times.

13-14: Accent your right thumb over your right shoulder two times.

15-16: Accent your left thumb over your left shoulder two times.

156. HAND TO FOREHEAD DRAMATIC POSE — Leaning the direction of the hand that you are using, bring the back of that hand to your forehead as if you are about to swoon. This melodramatic pose is a comical way of expressing distress, worry, sorrow, etc.

HAND TO FOREHEAD DRAMATIC POSE

157. HAND TO HEART — Hold your open hand (usually the right) to your heart with the palm facing your chest, as if you are reciting the "Pledge of Allegiance." This is a devoted pose of love and/or patriotism.

158. HAND TO FOREHEAD ala "SWOON" — A melodramatic pose in which the dancer brings their hand to their forehead as if they are about to faint. Lean far to the direction of the hand that you are using for a broader and more comic effect.

159. HANDS CHEST-UP (ONE AT A TIME OR BOTH) — This is a two-count gesture with your hands and arms. The hand(s) simply touches the chest area and then reaches to the ceiling. It is a very effective way to accent an "and one" feeling preceding a lyric.

160. HANDS TO CHEST — This move would suggest that the dancer place the fingertips of the hands at about chest level, perhaps touching, or at least very close to doing so.

161. HANDS TO HEART LEAN — A melodramatic pose. Place feet apart and then lean to the left so that all of the weight is on the left foot. The right leg is straight and the foot pointed. The hands are clasped at the heart. This can of course be performed to the right as well with all of the weight going onto the right foot. It is a pose suggesting "pining" or expressing love.

HANDS TO HEART LEAN

162. HANDS UP ala "SURRENDER" — Both hands are held overhead, slightly bent at the elbow with palms out toward the audience. This is like a captive prisoner "surrendering" to the authorities.

163. "HANG LOOSE" HANDS FROM LOW TO HIGH — "Hang Loose" is a comment heard frequently on the islands of Hawaii. It is accompanied by a hand gesture that consists of the thumb and little finger extended while the other fingers are curled into a fist position. "From low to high" would suggest that you scoop that hand position from low and by your sides to high overhead. This gesture would be used with surfing or beach-type music.

164. HEEL DRAGS — A bit of a misnomer in that the "heel" is not being dragged so much as the whole of the opposite foot. It is a country or folk-type step that begins by stepping onto the heel of one foot with the toes in the air, then pulling the opposite foot along so that the feet come together. In other words, the pattern of this walking pattern is step (heel), "drag" in opposite foot. You will recognize this step as one often used in Country line dancing.

HEEL DRAGS: see also 75. *Country Heel Drags*

165. HEEL GOES OUT, WITH JAZZ HANDS AND RIBCAGE ISOLATIONS (HOUND DOG) — To prepare for this routine, stand with slightly bent knees and jazz hands toward your own chest. Elbows are held quite high so that the lower part of the arm is parallel to the floor. On beat 1 extend your right foot with the toes up and the heel on the ground out to your right side. At the same time both of the jazz hands move so that they are spread out to your sides. The elbows remain close to your body at the ribcage. On beat 2 return to the starting position. On beat 3 repeat the same move out to the left side with the left foot extending and both hands again spread out to the sides. Repeat this sequence as many times as is indicated. An interesting pattern for this is R L R R L R L L. The "HOUND DOG" reference is due to the fact that this is a very similar move to those that Elvis Presley's dancers used to use when dancing to his hit *"You Ain't Nuthin' but a Hound Dog."*

HEEL GOES OUT, WITH JAZZ HANDS AND RIBCAGE ISOLATIONS (HOUND DOG)

166. HESITATION WALTZ — Like a regular waltz, this dance utilizes three whole counts. The difference is that on a regular waltz the dancers step three times, once for each quarter note. In a HESITATION WALTZ, the dancers take the first two steps only and then hold still for the third. You can think of it as quarter note followed by a half. You might also see it in a Minuet.

167. HIGH PRESENT FEET IN FIRST — Feet are together, hands are overhead in either jazz, blade or some other position usually specified.

HIGH PRESENT FEET IN FIRST

168. HIGH PRESENT FEET IN SECOND — Feet are apart, hands are overhead in either jazz, blade or some other position usually specified.

169. HIP ISOLATIONS — This instructs the dancer to move their hips (and their hips only) either forward and back, side to side, in circles or in any combination thereof.

170. not on video

170. HIP LIFTS — A relatively simple lift in which one dancer lifts their partner off the floor and onto their hip. This could be accomplished with hands in ballroom dance position, or with the man's hand around the woman's waist while the woman puts her arm around the shoulders of the man. The woman's feet are usually in a "back attitude" position or curled up near her chest. Keep in mind that in most lifts both partners are carrying their share of the load through leverage and timing.

H

HIP LIFTS

HIPS: see also *103. Facing Downstage R Accent Hips LRL RLR*

171. HIT HEEL ala CHARLESTON — With knees together kick one foot back and out to the same side. (For instance, the right foot out to the right side and somewhat back.) Slap the heel of that foot with the same hand while it is in the air. The slap would usually take place on the offbeat, or the "and" of the beat.

HIT HEEL ala CHARLESTON

172. HIT L HEEL WITH R HAND — Standing erect, the dancer brings the foot up to meet the hand either in front or behind the opposite leg. This specific direction calls for the left heel to be slapped by the right hand. You would generally get a more specific direction that would indicate where the hitting ought to occur.

173. HIT L LEG — If this were the only direction given it would generally mean that you are to slap the thigh of your left leg with your left hand. A more specific direction might include, "HIT L LEG WITH R HAND", or some other variation.

174. HIT R LEG — If this were the only direction given it would generally mean that you are to slap the thigh of your R leg with your R hand.

175. HITCH HIKE — A dance gesture born out of the 1960s. The dancer simply sticks out their thumb perhaps accenting it on each beat moving it across the front of their body from one side to the other at about waist level. To make it more physical, bend one knee and bounce a hip as you accent the thumb either with your feet together or apart.

176. HITCH KICKS — A HITCH KICK is in fact two kicks that make up one step. The first is a small kick to the front followed by a very high kick with the opposite foot. There are no steps in between so that the higher second kick has actually already begun before the first kick is ended. This athletic maneuver is great for Country Dances, or Can-Cans, but can also be used to simulate a sort of Kung Fu look.

HITCH KICK: see also *330. Running Hitch Kicks*

177. HOLD CHEEKS AND LOOK SHOCKED AT AUDIENCE..."HOME ALONE" — A gesture borrowed from the hit movie, the dancer places both hands on the sides of their face and either silently or audibly opens their mouth like a loud "AYE!" Use this funny gesture to show surprise or shock.

HOLD CHEEKS AND LOOK SHOCKED AT AUDIENCE... "HOME ALONE"

178. HOLD CHOIR BOOK, TURN THE PAGE — With both hands held together, palms up at about chest level, pretend to be holding a book of music. On a given count, cross your left hand over the top and pretend to flip a page. A fun gesture for a caroling choir or madrigal group spoofing themselves.

179. HOLD HEAD TILT L R — Hold onto the sides of your head as if it is aching and tilt from side to side. The move may suggest that you are listening to something or that you have a headache.

180. HOLD LAPELS ROCK FROM WAIST — In a very formal fashion, hold onto the lapels of your coat or vest (real or imaginary) and tilt from side to side at waist level. Usually the elbows should be held quite high, at least parallel to the floor.

181. HOLD LAPELS ROCK ON HEELS — Holding onto the lapels of your coat or vest (real or imaginary), keep your feet and legs firmly together as you rock on your heels and all of your toes go back and forth in the same direction. Generally this takes about two beats to rock from each side to side. (In other words, "half note rocks.")

HOLD LAPELS ROCK ON HEELS

182. HOLD BOTH HANDS WITH PARTNER — Face partner and hold both hands.

183. HOLDING BOTH HANDS, TURN WOMEN UNDER SO COUPLES ARE HUGGING BACK TO FRONT — A popular couples' move in which the dancers are holding both hands and facing each other. The male dancer lifts the hands bringing one pair of held hands over the other as the female turns under those upper hands. The couples end up with the same held hands but the female has her back to the male dancer in a come-from-behind hug. Do not let go of hands throughout the maneuver.

H

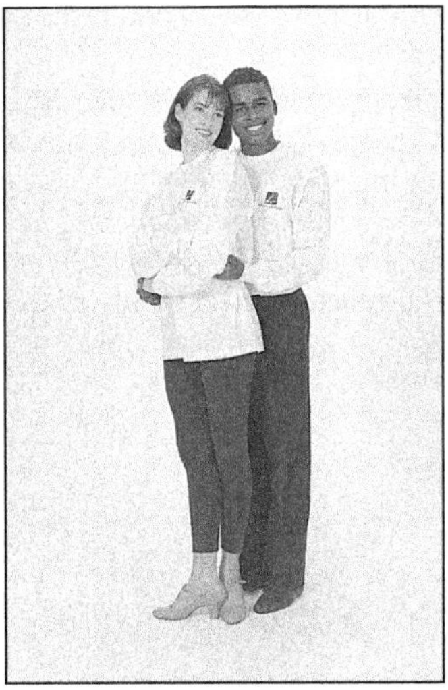

HOLDING BOTH HANDS,
COUPLES ARE HUGGING BACK TO FRONT

184. HOLDING HANDS FACING PARTNER TURN ALL THE WAY UNDER — The dancers face each other holding onto both hands. Then they turn toward the audience so that they duck under their own arms, turn so that they are back to back, and continue turning so that after one complete revolution they are back to facing each other. Hands are held throughout.

HOME ALONE: see *177. Hold Cheeks and Look Shocked at Audience...Home Alone*

185. HOOK THUMBS IN BELT LOOP — A hand posture with a decidedly Country or Nautical bend, the dancers simply loop their thumbs through their belt loops in front, or stick their thumbs into the waistband of their costume.

186. HOP BACK AND SNAP IN FRONT — Generally associated with Jitterbug or Lindy style dances, the dancer jumps back on themself with feet apart, leaning forward slightly from the waist. Jump with one foot first followed quickly by the other so that it has an "and 1" feeling. On beat 2 the dancer snaps the fingers of both hands in front, with wrists crossed at about chest level.

HOP BACK AND SNAP IN FRONT

187. HOP FORWARD AND SNAP BEHIND BACK — This move would very often follow the previously defined move (see above) in Jitterbug or Lindy style dances. Now the dancer hops forward in the same sort of "and 1" rhythm, but this time with feet together. As the hands go to snap behind the back on beat 2, the hips of the dancer will automatically jut forward.

HOP FORWARD AND SNAP BEHIND BACK

188. HOP IN CIRCLE CLAPPING THREE TIMES ON 2 3 4 — Hopping on both feet at the same time and making one complete revolution around yourself, you actually hop four times to make the circle clapping only on beats 2, 3 and 4. This is a more modern step used in Hip Hop and rock-type music.

189. HOP IN CIRCLE ON L FOOT — One circle around yourself, hopping three or four times to make one revolution. This might be done in a slower song and dance, perhaps soft shoe style.

HOP: see also *392. Straight Leg Hops Swinging Legs from Side to Side*

HOUND DOG: see *165. Heel Does Out, with Jazz Hands and Ribcage Isolations*

190. HUG PARTNER FRONT TO BACK — With both partners facing the same way, one of them (usually the male) is holding the crossed arms of the other. It is a very friendly pose.

191. HUG SELF — Cross your arms over your chest or stomach as if you are cold.

192. HUG SELF ala "RAP" — Blade hand crossed over chest and into the opposite armpit. Or, one of the arms may hold onto your chin between the thumb and forefinger while the other is crossed over stomach. This pose indicates a decidedly "bad" attitude which at the time it was popular (in the early 1990s) was decidedly "good."

193. HULA — A beautiful and flowing dance from the islands of Hawaii that utilizes waving arms and swaying hips.

I

194. INSIDE TURN — A pirouette in which the dancer spins around going left on the left foot, or right on the right foot.

195. INTERSECTING LINES — Two lines of dancers move so that the front line becomes the back and the back line becomes the front. Note that it is a movement and not just a position.

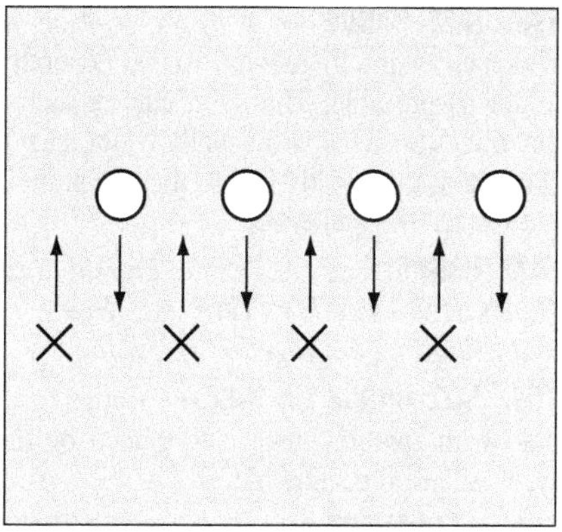

INTERSECTING LINES

196. ISOLATIONS — This would suggest that the dancer move whichever part of the body is indicated and that part **only**. In most cases this will involve the hips, the head, the shoulders or the chest.

J

197. not on video

197. JAMES CAGNEY, STRAIGHT-LEGGED WALK — A walk made famous by the performer who first portrayed George M. Cohan on stage. The dancer bends slightly forward from the waist, keeping their legs very stiff and straight, while taking quite large steps, mostly walking high on the balls of their feet.

JAMES CAGNEY, STRAIGHT-LEGGED WALK

198. JAZZ HANDS — A hand position in which all of the fingers are spread generally as far as possible. The palm can be facing any direction. That will usually be indicated. If it is not, it probably means that the palm is out toward the audience.

JAZZ HANDS: see also *289. Present Jazz Hands High* and *434. Turn Jazz Hands in and Bring Fingers Together Overhead*

199. JAZZ HANDS ON HIPS — Entire hand held with spread fingers and placed on the front side of the same hip.

200. JAZZ SQUARE — A dance pattern that is synonymous with a BOX STEP. It consists of four steps and can begin on any count of a measure to give it a variety of emphasis. (1) Step straight ahead with your left foot. (2) Step across the front with your right foot. (3) Step back and slightly left with the left foot. (4) Step out to the right with the right foot. During the entire four steps the shoulders are square to the way you were originally facing. Of course, this can be executed by beginning with the right foot and crossing the left as well.

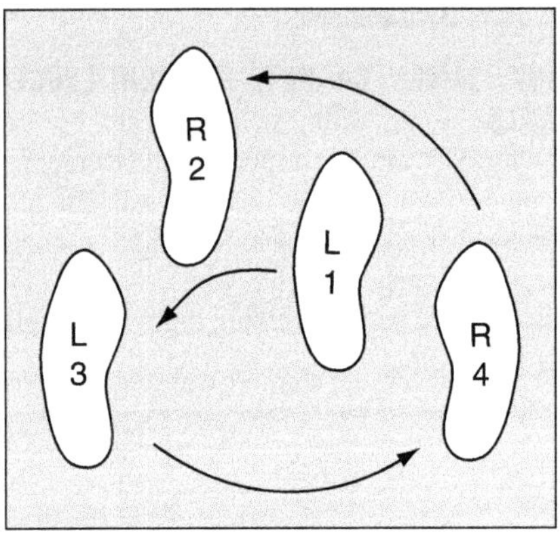

JAZZ SQUARE

JERK: see *413. The Jerk*

201. JIG/GIGUE — A Scottish/Irish and French dance with many similarities. The basic JIG involves hopping to the left followed by two quick steps (RL), then hopping to the right followed by two more quick steps (LR). The hands are held either both on the hips, both arched overhead, or one of each.

JIG/GIGUE

202. JIMMY DURANTE WALK — A walk made famous by this great American comedian with a famously large snozzola (nose). He would hold his hat slightly off from his head in his upstage hand (away from the audience). As he walked his chugging and halting walk, he would shimmy the hat as well as his head and nose.

JIMMY DURANTE WALK

203. JITTERBUG 6-COUNT — A traditional dance pattern that can be performed with or without a partner. It consists of a step (L), ball change (R L), step (R), ball change (LR), back step (LR).This would be counted "1 and 2, 3 and 4, 5 6." If you started the dance on beat 1 of four 4-beat measures, the accented L foot will be on a different beat of each ensuing measure until you have made an entire round. If this is performed in a traditional partnered ballroom dance formation, the female partner would begin the combination stepping onto the right foot.

204. JITTERBUG 8-COUNT — This is a variation of the traditional 6-count Jitterbug (see above) that simply adds two even walking steps after the backstep to make the combination a full 8 counts. This is often preferable when singing and dancing at the same time because the accented left foot will always occur on the downbeat of a measure.

205. JITTERBUG 8-COUNT WITH SPIN AWAY FROM PARTNER — In a ballroom dance position, the partners execute an 8-count Jitterbug (see above). The only variation occurs on beats 7 and 8 when the partners release their grip on each other and spin around themselves in one complete revolution so that they wind up facing each other again. The female spins to her right, the male to his left.

206. JITTERBUG COUPLES — This would suggest a traditional ballroom dance position with the male's left hand holding the female's right, his hand on the back of her waist, her left on the back of his right shoulder. Sometimes the female's right hand is actually placed on top of the male's index finger so that he can clasp her hand with his forefinger and thumb. This is a good position for the male to lead the dance and its many variations.

207. not on video

207. JITTERBUG SOLO — This means performing the traditional Jitterbug steps (see above), originally meant for a couple, as a solo dance.

208. JITTERBUG STYLE JUMP BACK CLAP — Generally associated with Jitterbug or Lindy style dances, the dancer jumps back on himself with feet apart, leaning forward slightly from the waist. Jump with one foot first followed quickly by the other so that it has an "and 1" feeling. On "2" the dancer claps his hands in front at about chest level.

209. JOHN TRAVOLTA HAND POINT (SATURDAY NIGHT FEVER) — A pose made famous by the actor John Travolta in the movie Saturday Night Fever. Associated with Disco dance, the performer points the right index finger into the air, with right hand on hip and both feet pointing to the right, with the heel of the right foot slightly off the floor.

JOHN TRAVOLTA HAND POINT (SATURDAY NIGHT FEVER)

210. JUMP STRAIGHT UP ARMS OVERHEAD — Like a Superman take-off, the performer pushes off the floor with one foot and jumps straight up with arms stretched straight overhead and toes pointed.

JUMP STRAIGHT UP ARMS OVERHEAD

K

211. KICK BALL CHANGE — Kick one foot followed immediately by two quick steps. For instance, if you kick the right foot, you follow it by stepping on the "ball" of that same foot and then transferring the weight onto the left foot.

212. KICK BALL CHANGE STEP FORWARD CLAP — A 4-count combination that begins with a KICK BALL CHANGE (see above) and is followed by a step forward with the kicked foot on beat 3. Then, on beat 4, the other foot steps up to join the originally kicked foot. Clap your hands as the feet come together.

213. KICKLINE (KNEE R KICK R, ETC.) — In the tradition of a high strutting kickline, this move breaks the kick into a four-step sequence. (1) Step with the left foot. (2) Bend the right leg up toward the chest. (3) Straighten that right leg out and point the right foot across the dancer's body towards downstage left. (4) Return the right leg to the bent position you had in step 2. (5) Step onto the right foot in order to begin the sequence to the other side.

214. KNEE/KICK — This is simply an abbreviated version of the above definition. Or it may indicate a step kick where the leg is never fully straightened. (In other words, step-knee.)

KNEE DRAGS: see *355. Single Knee Drags*

215. KNEE POPS FEET IN FIRST — Standing with your feet in first position (heels together and toes apart) lift your heels off the floor so the knees pop out and apart. Note that your head and shoulders stay at the same level throughout.

KNEE POPS FEET IN FIRST

216. KNEE POPS FEET IN SECOND — Standing in second position (feet apart) lift your heels off the floor so the knees pop out and apart. Note that your head and shoulders stay at the same level through out.

KNEE POPS FEET IN SECOND

L

217. L = left

218. "L" ARMS — A position of the arms in which they form the letter "L." One arm is toward the ceiling and one is parallel to the floor at shoulder level.

"L" ARMS

LASSO: see *405. Swinging a Lasso*

219. LAY-OUT — With one foot on the floor, the dancer stretches their body to its fullest extent so that it is parallel to the floor. Arms can be stretched out as well, also parallel to the floor. This move can be performed forward, sideways, or with a back bend.

LAY-OUT (FORWARD)

LAY-OUT (BACK BEND)

220. LEAN L — Lean to the left. This will usually be seen in reference to an entire cast, such as in a song where you want everyone swaying in the same direction.

221. LEAN R — Lean to the right. This will usually be seen in reference to an entire cast, such as in a song where you want everyone swaying in the same direction.

222. LEAN R, HAND TO EAR — Lunge or lean your entire body to the right with your right hand to your right ear as if you are listening to something in that direction.

223. LIFT CLASPED HANDS — Clasped hands with fingers intertwined or cupped together as if in prayer. Lift them from chest level to overhead.

224. LIFT R LEG ACROSS FRONT IN 3 — A "sweeping of the leg" move where the entire right leg is brought across the front of the body using a full three counts to reach its fullest height. This would usually be used in a waltz style dance with either a pointed or flexed foot.

LIFT R LEG ACROSS FRONT IN 3

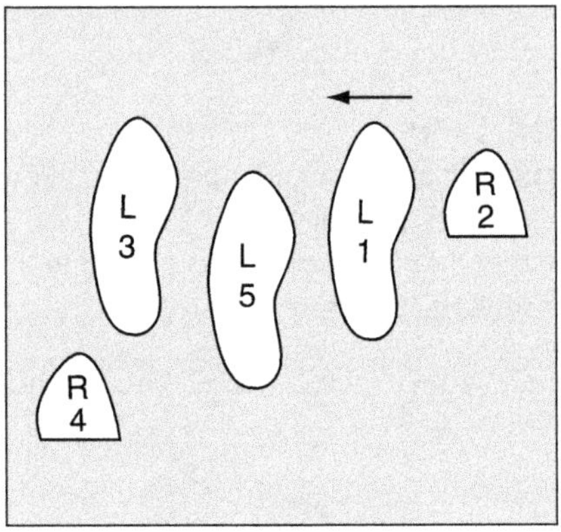

LINDY

225. LIFTS — This would refer to any maneuver where one dancer or group of dancers lifts another.

LIFTS: see also *19. Baby Carriage Lift, 126. Flip From Baby Carriage Lift, 170. Hip Lifts, 348. Shoulder Lift, 391. Straddle Lift Around Man's Waist, 416. Thigh Lift Girl's Feel Toward the Ceiling,* and *418. Three-Person Shoulder Lift*

226. LINDY — A five-step move associated with swing music. A basic Lindy step consists of a Chassé followed by a backstep. For instance, slide to the left in a dotted eighth-sixteenth-quarter pattern (LRL) and then a two quarter note backstep (RL), keeping your shoulders square to the audience the entire time. Repeat the pattern to the other side. This can also be performed with a partner. Face each other and either hold both hands or assume a ballroom dance position as you Lindy in the same direction.

L

LINDY: see also *261. Partnered Lindys*

227. LINK ELBOWS — Two dancers hook themselves together by intertwining their elbows. They could be facing each other and skipping around in circles such as in a Square Dance. In this case they would both be using the same arm. Or they could be facing the same direction, using opposite elbows as though they were walking arm-in-arm down the street together. There are also times when a longer line of dancers would link their elbows together as in a kick line situation.

228. not on video

228. "LOLLIPOP KIDS" STEP/JERK — This is a STEP TOUCH routine that was made famous by the Munchkins in the movie, The Wizard of Oz. The "Lollipop Kids" were three tough guys who would step one direction with the whole of one foot and then do a "touch" with the other, turning the toes out on that touching foot. In a sense, this is very similar to a GOSPEL STYLE STEP TOUCH except there is a much stronger accent on the "touch" that is backed into.

229. LOOK AT AN IMAGINARY RAINBOW FROM L TO R — This is a focus pattern which instructs the dancer or dancers to let their head and eyes arch from stage left to stage right in a huge arch as if they were following the arch of a rainbow from end to end. This is a simple and powerful focus tool which could have many variations but will center the energy of the cast and audience toward the sky.

230. LUNGE — Throwing your weight one direction or another. Usually the dancer bends the leg that is foremost in the direction you are lunging.

LUNGE

231. LUNGE R or LUNGE L — This is simply a more specific direction for the dancer in regards to their lunge. It might also suggest that the dancer "lunge downstage left," "lunge upstage right," "lunge directly downstage leading with your left foot," or some other such move.

M

232. MAJOR WHACK ATTACK — This is a fun name for any series of claps and slaps that constitute a body percussion routine. Usually a MAJOR WHACK ATTACK includes at least eight counts to the pattern. One simple "whack attack routine" would be:

1	clap
2	slap your R leg with your R hand
3	slap your L leg with your L hand
4	clap
5	hit your L heel with your R hand
6	slap your L leg with your L hand
7	slap your R leg with your R hand
8	clap
9	slap your L cheek with your L hand (not too hard!)
10	slap your R cheek with your R hand (not too hard!)
11	slap your L leg with your L hand
12	slap your R leg with your R hand
13-16	clap four times with each clap getting higher

233. MARCH — This simply instructs the dancer to walk to the beat of the music. It usually would suggest that the walk is a bit stronger than your usual stride, more like a soldier would walk to a cadence. It also suggests one step for each beat of the measure. A March tempo is generally assumed to be approximately quarter note = 120.

MARCH: see also *152., Half Time March, 371. Spirit of '76 March, 389. Stop March* and *390. Stop March Four-Point Pivot*

234. MARCH CLOG R L (RLR) L R (LRL) ETC. — Marching with a rhythmic pattern and intensity that would constitute a "clogging" dance. Clogging is seen in a lot of country and folk dance. This very basic CLOG routine instructs the dancer to complete this pattern: step, step, step ball change, step, step, step ball change, in a total of eight counts.

235. MARCH LIKE LITTLE KIDS — March with great energy picking your knees up almost as high as they can go and working your arms and fists in opposition with tremendous energy and enthusiasm. As you step on your left foot, your right fist swings back and so on.

236. MARCH MILITARY STYLE — A more rigid march that reflects the discipline of the military. Arms will generally be working with 90-degree bends at the elbow, one step on each beat.

237. MASHED POTATO — A silly dance of the 1950s and '60s in which the dancer keeps their knees together and elbows bent like the wings of a chicken. As the dancer flaps their elbows, they step down with one foot or the other as if they are "mashing potatoes" into the floor. Remember that the knees are together during this routine so it is only the lower part of the leg that is doing the bending and smashing. A common and interesting pattern for the MASHED POTATO is to mash four times with the right foot, then four with the left, followed by two right, two left, then one a piece four times R,L,R,L.

MASHED POTATO

238. MEAT GRINDER (INTERSECTING LINES) — This is a group action that has two or more lines intersecting each other like the tongs of a meat grinder. The back line of two parallel lines should be moving in and out of the windows of the row in front of them. One pattern has the dancers take four steps to switch places so that the rear line is now in front and vice versa. Four more steps in the opposite direction places the dancers back to their original spots. Then you can have the dancers move four steps side-to-side in the opposite direction of the other row. To the audience there will be the effect of lines crossing each other even though they do not actually intersect.

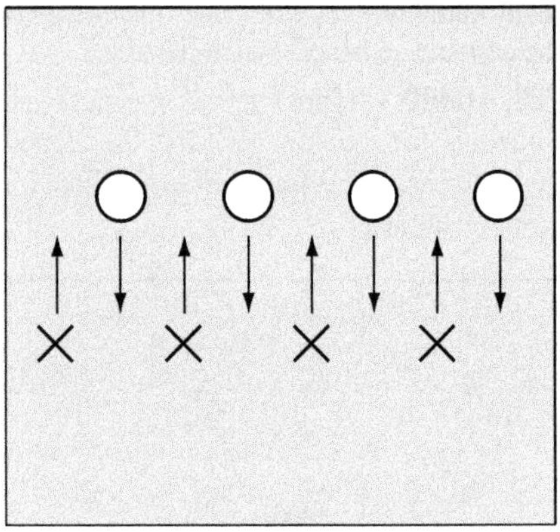

MEAT GRINDER (INTERSECTING LINES)

239. MEN OFFER GIRLS YOUR ELBOW — As if you are preparing to go for a walk, the gentleman holds up his bent elbow to his partner suggesting by this action that she link her arm in his.

240. MEN PULL GIRLS THROUGH LEGS ala CHARLESTON — Holding onto the girl's hands or wrists, the male dancer swings his leg over her head as she ducks. With her help, he then pulls her through his legs, heels first so that she ends up standing on the other side of him. This type of move was very popular in the hey day of Charleston and Varsity Drag, but continued to be used throughout the days of Jitterbug, Lindy and even in the Disco era.

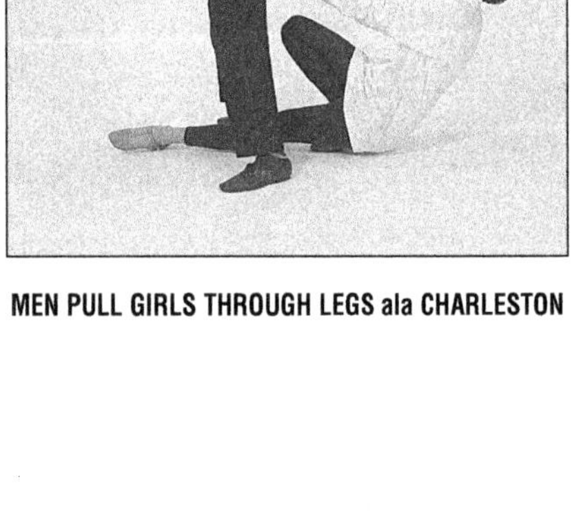

MEN PULL GIRLS THROUGH LEGS ala CHARLESTON

M

241. MEN PULL WOMEN OVER BACK IN A FULL FLIP — Stand facing your partner, holding both hands or wrists. Turn halfway around so you are standing back-to-back with held hands at shoulder level. The man bends his knees slightly, with feet apart, so that the small of his back is under the buttocks of the woman. The woman then tucks her legs toward her chest and pulls on the arms of the man so that she is lifted off the ground and onto the man's back. The man then pulls her over his head in a complete somersault and holds onto her hands until she is standing on the floor facing him again.

MEN PULL WOMEN OVER BACK IN A FULL FLIP

242. MICHAEL JACKSON SPIN — Any variation of a spin around oneself made famous by the pop star, Michael Jackson. An example is to cross your right foot over your left on beats "and 1" then swivel around to the left in two or three more counts, tucking your elbows in close to your sides and using a combination of heel/toe weight changes with each foot to help you get around.

243. MINOR WHACK ATTACK — A four or eight-count combination of slaps and claps that makes for an interesting body percussion routine. An example would be:

1 clap
2 slap your R leg with your R hand
3 slap your L leg with your L hand
4 clap
5 hit your L heel with your R hand
6 slap your L leg with your L hand
7 slap your R leg with your R hand
8 clap

244. MINUET HOLDING R HANDS — Facing your partner, place the female's right hand on top of the male's right hand. Utilizing a hesitation waltz pattern, step touch moving together and then apart like an old fashioned Minuet. This is a very formal dance. The women could hold their skirt with their free hand, and the men could place their free hand behind their back or hold the lapel of their jacket.

MINUET HOLDING R HANDS

245. MINUET HOLDING UPSTAGE HAND — A variation of the traditional Minuet, this dance utilizes the same hesitation Minuet pattern of stepping together and then apart once per measure. The only difference is that the dancers each use their upstage hand (one person's right, the other's left) instead of crossed hands to hold onto one another. This type of Minuet often works well for dancers who must also sing, as it leaves you more open to the audience than the traditional cross-handed Minuet.

M

246. MONKEY — A comical dance from the 1960s in which the dancers imitate actual monkeys by swinging their straight arms up and down like a monkey climbing a tree. In variations, some dancers have been known to actually pretend to peel a banana or scratch their flea-ridden bodies.

MONKEY

N

247. NOD (DOWN ON BEAT) — A simple piece of head choreography in which the dancer accents the beat of the music with a strong nod of the head, with the chin furthest down on the strongest part of the beat.

O

248. OFFSTAGE — The area of the auditorium or staging area that is not seen by the audience. This would include the wings, dressing areas, green rooms, etc.

249. OPEN FIST, DROP HAND — A move that resembles the freeing of a captive bird in which the dancer lifts their fist above their head and then opens it fully as if releasing their captive. It is a simple and effective gesture that suggests *freedom, flight, hope, or even dreams.*

250. OPEN HAND SLOWLY AS IF RELEASING A BIRD OR A DREAM ("FREE") — Same as previous definition. (See above.)

251. "OPERA" HANDS — Holding your hands clasped together at chest level in a caricature-like imitation of a formal opera singer or recitalist. One hand is on top of the other, clasped together with fingers to the inside of the opposite hand's knuckles.

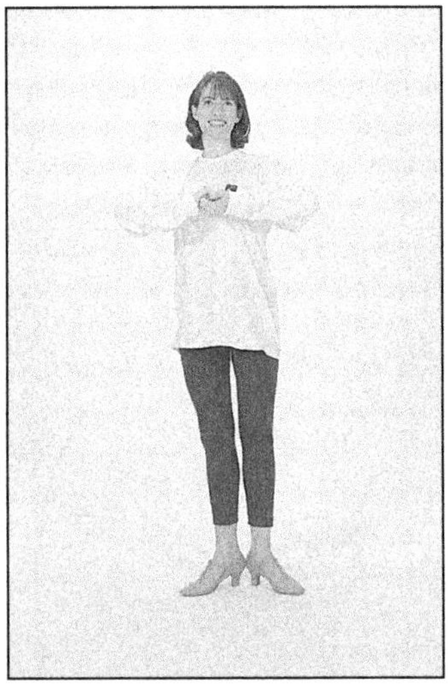

"OPERA" HANDS

252. OUTSIDE TURN — A spin or pirouette in which the dancer turns to the right on their right foot or to the left on their left foot.

253. "OY VEY" HEAD RAP — A comical gesture that suggests forgetting something or being flabbergasted by something. The dancer taps their forehead with the heel of their hand and rolls their eyes as if to say "oy vey!" or "how could I forget that?"

"OY VEY" HEAD RAP

P

254. PADDLEWHEEL TURN — A series of step ball changes (usually four steps and three ball changes) that propel the dancer in a circle around oneself. It is almost as if one foot is nailed to the floor and the other is trying to go someplace. The result is that you move in circles. Recognized mostly in soft shoe style dances, the Paddlewheel turn can be adapted to almost any style or period from Country to Conga, Charleston to Jazz! The arms are often held straight in a diagonal pattern with the arm down the direction the dancer is turning.

PADDLEWHEEL TURN

255. PATTY CAKE — A partnered routine that resembles the child's game by the same name. One pattern is as follows (facing your partner):

1 slap your legs
2 clap
3 hit right hands together
4 clap
5 hit left hands together
6 clap
7 hit both hands together
8 clap

256. PANTOMIME PIANO PLAYING — With slightly curled fingers, the dancer pretends to play the piano. One pattern is to simply let the parallel hands "play" two pulses left and two pulses right, or one apiece, at about waist level.

257. PARTNER-LESS TANGO — Extend one arm straight out in front of you at about shoulder level. The other hand is placed at about chest level with a bent elbow parallel to the floor. The dancer dramatically walks four steps toward the direction of the straight arm, then switches arms so that the other is straight and go in that direction for four steps. It's as if you are doing the Tango dance but are not bothering to wait for a partner.

PARTNER-LESS TANGO

P

258. PARTNER CARTWHEEL — One dancer executes a cartwheel using the legs (thighs) of the other dancer as the brace for their arms and hands as opposed to the floor. The standing partner can help guide the cartwheeler by holding their waist as they pass over.

259. PARTNER CHARLESTON — Holding your partner in a traditional ballroom dance position, you each do a series of step touches that move one forward and then one back, always in opposition. This is a very lively dance from the early part of the century.

PARTNER CHARLESTON

260. PARTNERS IN DANCE POSITION STEP KICK THROUGH EACH OTHER'S LEGS — Facing your partner and holding either both hands or a ballroom dance position, the dancers step on the beat and kick their other foot through the legs of their partner on the offbeat. This works especially great in Charleston, or swing numbers.

PARTNERS IN DANCE POSITION STEP KICK THROUGH EACH OTHER'S LEGS

261. PARTNERED LINDYS — Standing in ballroom dance position or facing each other and holding both hands, the dancers each slide or Chassé in one direction (for example, downstage) followed by a backstep. This can be repeated and embellished with turns, spins and new directions for a lively dance appropriate to the music of the 1940s to the 1960s.

262. PARTNERS STROLL ARM-IN-ARM — Linked together at the elbows and each facing the same direction, the dance couples walk about the stage as if walking through the neighborhood. Generally the upstage dancer will be a bit ahead so that the audience has a view of both dancers and voices can continue to project forward.

PARTNERS STROLL ARM-IN-ARM

P

PARTNER: see also *184. Holding Hands Facing Partner Turn All the Way Under* and *190. Hug Partner Front to Back*

263. PAS DE BOURRÉE — The French term for a three-step pattern that basically has one step going behind, the next almost in place, and the third back to second position. For instance, (1) step with the L foot as far to the right of the R foot as possible from behind, (2) step slightly forward with the R foot, and (3) step out to the left again with the L foot to resume your starting position, or lunge slightly to the left with that L foot.

264. PASSÉ — The French term for a two-part move. (1) Lift the knee across the front and up toward the waist, and (2) point that same foot that was lifted out to its own side.

265. PEEL OFF — Any move that is done by each member of the cast in succession, like the "Wave" a crowd does in a sports stadium. This move could be executed like the falling of a row of dominos by individuals or small groups perhaps on each beat of a measure, on the down beat or in some other even sequence.

PEEL OFF: see also *130. Four Group Peel Off*

266. PIGEON TOES — This would suggest either a stance or a movement in which the toes of both feet are turned in to face one another.

267. PINWHEEL — A group of dancers moving in a circle either in a waltz pattern or just walking. Sometimes they may be holding hands or wrists in the middle of the circle so that they resemble the spokes of a wheel.

PINWHEEL

268. PIVOT TO FACE BACK (1 POINT TURN) — An "about-face" in which the dancer steps directly toward the audience on beat 1 and then turns to face the back with a step on the opposite foot on beat 2. For instance, if the dancer steps downstage with their L foot, they will step on their R foot and turn to the right to face upstage for the second move.

PIVOT: see also *131. Four-Point Pivot, 437. Two-Point Pivot, 438. Two-Point Pivot Burst* and *439. Two-Point Pivot with Claps*

269. PLIÉ — The French term for bending your knees. It is considered the opposite of RELEVÉ.

Plié Relevé

PLIÉ/RELEVÉ

270. POINT — (A) Using your index or some other finger to indicate a direction. (B) A pivot spot on the floor as in a "two-point pivot." (C) A reference point in a move such as in a "three-point turn."

271. POINT R HAND L TO R — There would be obvious variations of this direction but an example would simply mean to "point your R hand from stage left to stage right, usually at about chest level." Other variations would include "point R hand R to L, point L hand R to L, point L hand L to R."

272. POINT R HAND LOW TO HIGH — Similar to the previous definition, there could be many variations to this instruction that are quite obvious. This particular direction uses the index finger to point from the floor to the ceiling.

P

273. POINTED FOOT — A more accurate way of instructing the dancers to use their entire foot to point as opposed to pointing "their toes." The whole foot works by extending the toes downward and the heel up. (*A hint to make the foot look even more pointed is to bring the heel of that foot forward as you point it, to get a longer more elegant line.*)

POINTED FOOT

274. POLKA — A dance familiar to European and Scandinavian folk dances, three steps and a hop make up a basic Polka step. It can be performed individually, in a traditional ballroom dance position with a partner, with elbows linked or with many other variations. This is generally considered a lively dance full of spins, covering considerable territory.

275. POLKA: HEEL TOE SLIDE — Facing the audience, the dancer touches the heel of the foot out to the side and then brings the same foot across and in front of the other and touches the toes to the floor. Following this heel and toe maneuver, the dancer slides or Chassés to the same side as the working foot. In other words, the L heel crosses the right, the L toe touches out to the left and then the dancer slides to the left in a "3 and 4" pattern.

276. PONY — Basically a Polka for the 1950s through 1970s, this is also a three-step pattern in which the dancer hops onto one foot and quickly follows with a ball change. There are many variations for the hands including holding the reins of an imaginary pony, pretending to swing a lasso, or even pretending to use a riding crop on your imaginary horse.

PONY

277. PONY AROUND SELF — Using the basic hop ball change of a Pony step, the dancer makes a complete circle around themself. They will usually use 4, 6, or 8 complete pony routines to make the revolution.

278. PONY WITH TRAVELING ARMS — Using the traditional Pony (hop ball change) pattern, the dancer incorporates the cranking or churning hand motions that a referee uses to call a "traveling" infraction in the game of basketball. This combination works wonderfully for dances of a Latin or Caribbean nature.

PONY WITH TRAVELING ARMS

POOH HIPS: see *109. Feet Apart, Swing Hips*

P

279. POUND FIST TO HEART — Simply take one fist and accent each beat of the music, or every couple of beats, by earnestly tapping the inside knuckles to your chest.

280. "PRAY" HANDS — Hold your straight hands together with the fingers pointed toward the ceiling as if you are in a position of prayer.

"PRAY" HANDS

281. "PRAY" HANDS/FINGERS INTERTWINED — Hold your hands together as if in a position of prayer, this time with your fingers interlaced.

"PRAY" HANDS/FINGERS INTERTWINED

282. PRESENT ARMS CHEST OUT — A two-part move that begins by bringing both hands close to your chest. Then reach both of those hands out toward the audience with straight arms as if you are "presenting" them. The palms will usually be up, but many variations could occur.

283. PRESENT ARMS — This definition is borrowed from game show models whose job it is to "present" the prizes behind revealing doors or curtains. They usually move their upturned palms with a straight arm across the space of the prize. (A) So if the direction is to "present the audience," the dancer may move their right hand from stage L to R at about chest level. (B) "Present arms" could also be a more stationary position. If the directions are to "present high," the dancer simply raises their straight arms overhead in a "Y" pattern. Usually, there will be a more specific direction as to the exact position of the hands. For instance, "present jazz hands low" would tell the dancer to extend both arms out to the sides, front and lower than the waist with spread fingers, palms out toward the audience. There are almost unlimited variations of "PRESENT ARMS."

PRESENT: see also *167. High Present Feet in First* and *168. High Present Feet in Second*

284. PRESENT ARMS DIAGONAL — This arm position suggests that the arms are held out straight with palms up, one low and one high so that they make a diagonal line.

PRESENT ARMS DIAGONAL

285. PRESENT BOTH HANDS FROM CHEST OUT TOWARD AUDIENCE — Hold your hands at chest level with palms up. Then move

P

them out and away from your body as if you are "presenting" the audience. This basic message is "from me to you."

286. not on video

286. PRESENT DANCE POSITION "DO YOU WANT TO DANCE?" — One dance partner holds up their hands at about chest level, with palms up and arms outstretched, as if to ask the other dancer if they would like to dance.

287. PRESENT FREE HAND, PALM DOWN SLIGHTLY OVERHEAD — This suggests that one hand is occupied, perhaps holding a partner's hand, or a prop. The other hand is extended overhead and out to the side with the palm down. It is an ending pose following a dance number or partner combination.

288. PRESENT HIGH WITH BENT WRISTS — Generally interpreted as a feminine pose, it need not necessarily be the case, however both arms are held straight and overhead like a capital letter "Y". The palms and the wrists are bent down as well.

PRESENT HIGH WITH BENT WRISTS

289. PRESENT JAZZ HANDS HIGH — Stretch both hands overhead so you look like a capital letter "Y". Your palms are out toward the audience with spread fingers.

290. PRESENT L HAND FROM R TO L AT CHEST LEVEL — With the palm up, the L hand only moves from stage R to L at about chest level. Obviously, there could be variations of this and the opposite can be done with the R hand moving from L to R.

291. PRESENT L HAND TO STAGE L — Reach your L hand and fully extended arm with the palm up toward downstage L at about chest level or slightly lower.

292. PRESENT L HAND TO STAGE R — Reach the L hand across your body at about chest level and with the palm up so that you are reaching toward downstage R.

293. PRESENT THE BAND WITH UPSTAGE HAND — This direction is to reach the hand that is closest to the band toward them with the palm up as if you are acknowledging their contribution to the production. This assumes that the band is set upstage of the dancers.

294. PRESS HANDS DOWN, PALMS DOWN — Move your hands from whatever position they are in toward the stage with the palms down. Create a sense of resistance as you lower them to give them a look of strength. For instance, move your hands from a "present high" toward the floor with palms down.

295. PRETEND TO DIVE — Exactly as it suggests, the dancers hold their hands overhead either with palms down or pressed together like praying hands. Pretend to take a headfirst leap from a diving board into a pool of water.

296. not on video

296. PRETEND TO DRIVE A CAR — With one or both hands on the top of an imaginary steering wheel, the dancers rock the hands in an arching pattern back and forth at about chest level as if you are steering a car. If you are only using one hand, the other could be held with a thumb in your belt loop or waist band, or around the shoulder of a partner/passenger.

PRETEND TO DRIVE A CAR

297. PRETEND TO ROW — The dancers make believe they are rowing or paddling a boat or canoe. This might mean that one foot is up on a riser as you "paddle" on one side of an imaginary canoe, or if you are sitting on the floor, both arms can rotate as if you are maneuvering a row boat.

298. PULL R FIST DOWN FOR CUT-OFF — Like a rock star, the singer pulls their open hand down to their chest. By the time it reaches their heart it is in a fist and is the signal for the music to cut off. Sometimes this is preceded by a huge jump and ends in a kneeling position.

PULL R FIST DOWN FOR CUT-OFF

299. PULSE FISTS AT SIDES — Bending your elbows at 90 degrees, accent your fists down on the beat. The knuckles of each hand are toward the ceiling. At almost any speed this move sends a very strong message of power and determination.

300. PULSE HIP FORWARD — Turn the side of one foot so that it is parallel to the audience, keeping your shoulders square or parallel to the audience as well. On the beat of the music, thrust the same hip forward as the foot that is forward and parallel. In other words if the R foot is forward, pulse the R hip toward the audience on the beat.

301. PULSE ON YOUR HEELS — This simply means that the dancer lifts their heels from the floor and sets them down so that they make contact with the floor on each beat. Basically, this is a series of relevés. The lifting of the heels can happen one of two ways; (1) lifting the heels off the floor with straight legs so that the entire body from head to toe is elevated or, (2) bending the knees so that the heels lift off the floor but the head stays at one elevation. (This type of heel pulse would usually be described as a "knee pop" rather than a pulse on the heel since the knees do the work and will be the most prominent feature of the move.)

302. PUNCH FIST FROM SHOULDER UP — A two-count move in which the dancer first holds the fist at shoulder level (i.e. right fist to right shoulder) and then punches it straight up in the air.

303. PUNCH FIST LOW ACROSS THE FRONT — A one-count move in which the dancer punches the fist at a diagonal across the body and down. For instance, when facing the audience, punch the right fist toward the floor slightly stage left of yourself.

304. PUNCH FIST UP — A one-count move in which the dancer punches their fist toward the ceiling. A powerful final pose or gesture of "power."

305. PUNCH R FIST ACROSS FRONT TO L — This would specifically suggest that the right fist punches across the front of a dancer who is facing the audience. This time the arm would be extended parallel to the floor at about shoulder height. This could also be performed with the left fist punching to the right.

P

PUNCH R FIST ACROSS FRONT TO L

306. PUSH FOOT OUT/TOGETHER — A funky two-count move that resembles the squishing of a bug out to the dancer's side. Facing the audience, on beat 1 the dancer pushes the foot directly out to the side utilizing the ball and toes of the foot only. As the dancer does this, their shoulders will turn away from that pushed foot. If the left foot is pushed out to the left, the shoulders will turn so that the upper body faces somewhat stage right. Only partial weight is put on that stepping foot with most of the weight remaining on the stationary leg. The second move brings that pushed foot back to its starting position (feet together) and shoulders again square to the audience. Try it to the other side and alternate it back and forth for a fun and funky dance routine.

PUSH FOOT OUT/TOGETHER

307. PUSH STEPS "SQUISH A BUG" — See above definition as these two instructions are essentially different ways of describing the same move.

R

308. R = Right

309. RAH! FIST ACROSS FRONT — Swing your fist across the front of your body at about waist level with the elbow bent at 90 degrees like a cheerleader as they accent their cheer.

RAH! FIST ACROSS FRONT

310. RAINBOW ARM — Using a straight arm with the palm down, make one complete rotation of that arm across the front of your body. The arm begins in a downward motion across the front, moves out to the opposite side, overhead and to the same side as the "moving" arm and back down to the side where it began. It is simply a 360 degree circle of the arm with the performer facing the audience the entire time. The "rainbow" analogy comes from the overhead arch that the arm and hand makes as it completes the top half of the rotation. It is an effective move when the dancer wants to accentuate lyrics about the *sky,* the *world, space, everything* or *everywhere,* etc.

RAINBOW: see also *63. Circle Rainbow Arm 360 Degrees, 64. Circle Right Arm (Rainbow Arm)* and *229. Look at an Imaginary Rainbow from L to R*

311. REACH HAND HIGH WITH FEET TOGETHER (ENDING POSE) — Use this for a strong and effective ending pose, like the Statue of Liberty. The reaching hand could either be a jazz hand, a fist, a point or outstretched fingers with the palm turned in or out from the body.

312. RELEVÉ — This is a French term that essentially means pushing up from your heels so that you are standing on the balls of your feet or even your tip toes. This is the opposite of plié.

313. RHUMBA (or Rumba) — A ballroom dance of Cuban origin in 2/4 or 4/4 time with a basic pattern of step-close-step, marked by a delayed transfer of weight and pronounced hip movements.

314. through 320. not on video

314. RIBCAGE ISOLATIONS FRONT BACK — The only thing that moves is the ribcage which moves forward and backward. You might use this along with walking knee pops or a Caribbean style dance. It is also a very good exercise and warm up routine.

315. RIBCAGE ISOLATIONS SIDE TO SIDE — The only thing that moves is the ribcage which moves side to side.

316. RIDING A HORSE, STRADDLE — With feet far apart, slightly bend your knees and bounce. You may want to accent the bounce by lifting your toes from the floor and then bouncing down on them for each beat. Hold your hands like they are holding the reins of a horse. A free hand could pretend to slap the saddle or even swing a lasso.

RIDING A HORSE, STRADDLE

317. RIPPLE KICKS ala "ROCKETTES" — In a long line, the dancers kick one leg straight out in front of them at about waist height or more. Like a row of falling dominos, the dancers kick their legs one right after the next to give the kick line a rippling, or peel off effect. This is the kind of trick witnessed often in routines performed by Radio City Music Hall's "Rockettes."

318. RIPPLE — Any move that is performed by a row or rows of dancers in a sequence. Like a row of dominos, one person does something immediately followed by the next as if the first caused the next. The "wave" that you see in a stadium full of people is an example of a "ripple." Sometimes this may be referred to as a fast peel-off.

319. RIPPLE STOP — This is when a group of dancers is performing a move or routine and one dancer abruptly stops, with the effect of this stop seeming to stop each of the dancers in sequence. An example would be if a row of penguins was walking and the front one stopped suddenly causing the next in line to run into them and stop, likewise the next and the next and the next until the entire row had stopped.

320. ROCK FROM HIPS — See ROCK FROM THE WAIST.

321. ROCK FROM THE WAIST — Tilting your upper body either side to side or front to back, or even at angles, with the bend happening at the waist. The lower body would remain stationary. Try it with your hands on your hips as an example.

322. ROCK HEADS SIDE TO SIDE — Tilt your head from side to side by lowering your ear toward the same shoulder. You can go directly from side to side or stop in the middle position (straight up) in between tilts.

323. ROCK IN DANCE POSITION — Couples in ballroom dance position simply rock side to side in unison. While holding hands (man's L woman's R), and woman's L hand on the man's shoulder and his R on her waist, face stage R and L respectively, and simply tilt from the waist downstage and upstage to the beat of the music.

ROCK IN DANCE POSITION

324. ROCK ON HEELS, FEET GO L R L R — With feet together and usually with hands behind back or on hips, keep the weight on your heels and swing the toes of your feet back and forth from stage left to right, left to right.

ROCK: see also *108. Feet Apart Rock Side to Side Slapping Thighs on 1 and 3*

325. ROCKING AND SLAP THIGHS ON 1 AND 3 — With feet apart, transfer your entire weight from one side to the other with knees slightly bent. Slap both thighs on the beats as you make the full transfer of weight. This would work in "country and western" music particularly, and especially for younger performers who may have a problem placing the thigh slaps on the appropriate offbeats. (See next definition.)

326. ROCKING AND SLAP THIGHS 2 and 4 — With feet apart, transfer your entire weight from one side to the other with knees slightly bent. Slap both thighs on the offbeats following the transfers of weight. This is an excellent "country and western" move.

327. RUBBER LEGS — Stand with your feet shoulder width apart and slightly bent knees with the weight on the balls of your feet. Flap your legs together and apart as if they were rubbery.

328. RUBBER LEGS WITH HANDS ON KNEES IN 1920s STYLE — Place your feet approximately shoulder width apart. Your knees are slightly bent and your hands are on your knees. Move your knees together, and as they touch, slide your hands so they switch knees as the knees go apart again. Repeat the knees coming together, and switch hands back so that as they go apart the second time, you are back to your original position. Repeat this quickly several times for an effective Charleston or Ragtime dance move.

RUBBER LEGS WITH HANDS ON KNEES IN 1920s STYLE

329. RUNNING FLAPS — A tap dance and soft shoe term. A "flap" means that you brush the toes of the foot on the floor as it moves away from your body and then immediately place weight on that same foot. The two parts of the move make a "fl—ap" sound. RUNNING FLAPS means that you do several of these in a row, alternating feet as though you were running, either in place or actually moving. The weight always remains on the balls of the feet throughout the running.

330. RUNNING HITCH KICKS — A HITCH KICK is when you kick one foot out in front of yourself not very high (about waist high), and follow that immediately with a very high kick of the other leg. RUNNING HITCH KICKS mean that you put at least two running steps before each hitch kick. The pattern would be run L, run R, kick L (not too high), kick R very high.

S

331. "S" POSE — In various degrees this is a stance in which the dancer's feet are together with one foot and leg slightly in front (downstage) of the other. The shoulders remain square to the audience so there is a natural "S" line that runs up the forward leg, across the hip, waist, chest and shoulder. The hands are held either on the hip, overhead, down at the sides or in some other variation. This is the traditional pose of showgirls, models or even body builders because it is a flattering stance on almost all types of bodies.

"S" POSE

332. "S" POSE BOP HIP — Standing in the "S" POSE (see above), bounce your hip so the accent is either down on the beat or up on the beat. This is a sassy move when performed at a quick tempo, and sultry move at slower tempos.

333. "S" POSE ARMS OVERHEAD — Standing in an "S" POSE (see above) arms are extended high overhead with palms up or down. Shoulders are square to the audience as if you are balancing a huge headdress upon your head.

334. SALUTE — The right hand with palm down and fingers together, is brought to the forehead just above the eyebrow with the elbow held out to the side. A "Gomer Pyle" salute would turn the hand out so that the palm is facing the audience. This is named after the famous television character made famous by Jim Nabors. Others may call it the "Dudley Do-Right" salute after another fictional character.

SALUTE: see also *417. Three-Count Salute*

335. SCOOP FIST — Bring your fist from down at your side to overhead with the arm straight and the knuckles up.

336. SCOOP BOTH HANDS — With palms up, bring your straight arms from low by the sides of your leg to overhead. It's as if you are scooping up something or lifting something to overhead.

337. SCOOP BOTH HANDS FROM CHEST LEVEL TO OVERHEAD — Both hands are held straight out and slightly spread at chest level with palms up. The direction instructs the dancer to lift both arms from this chest high position to overhead ending in a "Y" formation.

338. SCOOP BOTH HANDS FROM LOW TO HIGH — (See SCOOP BOTH HANDS.)

339. SCOOP HAND PALM UP — Scoop one hand which will most often be indicated L or R, from low by your side to overhead.

340. SCOOP HAND PALM DOWN LOW TO HIGH — Move your straight arm from low by your leg to any higher elevation with the palm facing the floor, fingers together and extended. This is a "wing-like" move indicative of flying, etc.

341. SECOND POSITION — Referring to how you are standing, SECOND POSITION means feet apart. On occasion there may be more specific direction such as "parallel second position" which would indicate that the feet should be pointed straight ahead and no further apart than the heels. A "turned out second position" would mean that the feet are apart with the toes actually further apart than the heels.

342. SHIM SHAM (FLIM FLAM) — This is a dance pattern associated with soft shoe and sand dancing. In this dance you put the whole of one foot out in front of you and then drag it back so it makes a stomp/drag sound (for example R). Follow this by doing the same with the other foot (L), and again with the original foot (R). Then add a quick ball change, step (RLR) pattern so you can begin the entire routine with the other foot (L). Each side takes 8 counts.

1	2	3	4
R	drag	L	drag

5	6	and	7	8
R	drag	L	R	drag
		(ball change)		

343. SHIMMY HANDS — With open hands (jazz hands), shake them without letting them lose their rigidity. You are shimmying your entire hand, not just wiggling the fingers.

344. SHIMMY JAZZ HANDS LIKE SNOW FALLING — With palms out toward the audience, shimmy the jazz hands from high to low, bending the elbows as the hands come from straight overhead down to your sides. This is suppose to suggest *falling snow.*

345. SHIMMY SHOULDERS — With shoulders square to the front, move them quickly forward and back in alternating pattern so they shimmy. It is often easier to do this if the dancer holds their elbows in quite closely to their sides with hands out slightly further in a "snapping" position.

346. SHOOT UP HANDS OVERHEAD UP DOWN UP DOWN "Celebrate" — A repetitive mood celebratory in nature in which the out-turned jazz hands go from shoulder height to fully extended on every other beat.

347. SHORTY GEORGE — A dance step made famous in the early part of the 1900s, the dancer steps across their front with their entire foot (R). The toes of that foot would face the opposite wall (L). Then they twist that foot on its heel so that the toes move back toward the right. It's as if the dancer is grinding something into the ground with their heel. Just remember to step twist step twist, with arms working in opposition to the feet.

SHORTY GEORGE

348. SHOULDER LIFT — This basic shoulder lift ends up with one partner of a dance couple (usually the female) sitting on one of the shoulders of her male partner. They are usually facing the same direction but there are variations that will have her sitting in the opposite direction as well. The girl's feet are both to the side that she is sitting on and the male is balancing her with his hand on her back and leg or on her back and holding one of her hands for leverage. A great stationary pose or a spinning dance position.

SHOULDER LIFT

349. SHRUG — Hold both hands with bent elbows at about ear level with palms up. Raise the shoulders slightly as if to ask a question.

350. SHRUG BACK TO BACK — A couple of dancers standing back to back and shrugging their hands and shoulders. Generally they will be slightly angled downstage as opposed to standing exactly back to back.

SHRUG BACK TO BACK

351. SHRUG L HAND or SHRUG R HAND — This is simply a more specific direction that has the dancer performing the shrug move as described above but with only one hand.

352. SHUFFLE BACK LIKE DOMINOS — This is a move in which a whole line of dancers facing the same direction shuffles their feet very rapidly and spreads out like an accordion. The "dominos" description unfolds in a cause and effect manner as one person's moves seem to cause the next to move.

353. SHUFFLE OFF TO BUFFALO — An old tap and soft shoe routine that is basically a running step (LRLRLRLRLR etc.) in which the shoulders are square to the audience. As the dancer steps onto their L foot, the heel of their R is lifted in front of the L leg. (A variation sometimes has the R heel being lifted behind the L leg.) This pattern is repeated over and over as the dancer moves toward stage L. It can then be reversed so that the R leg is doing the stepping and the L heel is lifted as the dancer shuffles off to stage R. The hands are usually held in a fist position on the hips or in front of the dancer with the fists pulling up on each heel lift. The "Shuffle" actually refers to the tap-like shuffle of the trailing foot as the leading foot is being stepped upon before the shuffling heel is lifted in front.

354. SIDE SADDLE — Pretend as though you are riding a saddled horse with both legs on one side of the horse. The knees are together and slightly bent. The shoulders are square to the audience as if you are watching where you are going. If this is a couple routine, the male dancer might be in front riding in a traditional "straddling the horse" posture, with the female "side saddle" behind him and holding onto his waist.

SIDE SADDLE

355. SINGLE KNEE DRAGS — Kneeling on one knee, the dancer steps forward with the other foot and then drags the knee up to meet it moving in the same direction.

356. SKATE — The dancers pretend to be ice skating or roller skating. To accentuate the move, as you step onto one foot lift the other behind in a 90 degree attitude. Hands can be held behind the back, inside a real or imaginary muff, or held in the hands of a partner.

SKATE: see also *135. Funky Skate Step-Axle*

357. SKIP — step hop, step hop, step hop, etc. like the playful run of a small child.

358. SLAP THIGHS (TRIPLETS) — With feet either apart or together, slap the top of the respective thighs with open hands in a triplet pattern (1 and a 2 and a 3 and a 4.)

359. "SLEEP HANDS" UNDER CHEEK — With hands held together like you are going to pray (extended fingers), place both hands under the cheek of your face and tilt your head slightly to that side as if your hands were a pillow.

360. SLICE R HAND FROM HIGH TO LOW ACROSS FRONT — From a position where your hand is extended, palm up, overhead and slightly to the side (for example R), bring that hand at a diagonal across the front of your body all the way to the floor stage L of where you are standing. The left knee will have to bend as the hand gets lower.

361. SLIDE L (SLIDE R) — Facing the audience, simply step to the left with the left foot and then bring the R foot along until they are back together. Reverse it so that you step R and drag the left foot to meet it.

362. SLIDE L WITH DIAGONAL ARMS (Fred Astaire) — Facing the audience, step to the left with the left foot extending, the left arm up and to the left as the right arm trails down and to the right. Slide R and extend the R arm up toward high stage R trailing with the left arm. In other words, the arm is higher the direction that you are moving. This is the kind of elegant move made famous by dancers like Fred Astaire and Ginger Rogers.

SLIDE L WITH DIAGONAL ARMS (Fred Astaire)

363. SLOW TWIST LEAN L (R) — While performing the Chubby Checker Twist (twisting the lower half of your body back and forth from the balls of your feet), lean slowly toward stage L for any number of counts. Then continue to twist and lean to the R for the same amount of counts.

SMURF: see *414. The Smurf.*

364. SNAKE (LEAD WITH HEAD) — A 1980s move in which the dancer ripples their entire body toward one side of the stage or the other beginning with the top of their head and isolating each part of the body so that it sequences all the way down to the feet. Usually it is performed with shoulders basically square to the audience. For instance, leaning toward the left, lunge with top of the head followed by L shoulder, L side of rib cage, L waist, L hips, L leg. Repeat to the right.

365. SOFT SHOE — A dance that is essentially tap dancing without the taps. In other words, soft soled shoes are used with similar dance steps and combinations of tap dancing.

SOFT SHOE: see also *25. Basic Soft Shoe* and *26. Basic Soft Shoe 337*

366. SOUPY SHUFFLE (LRLLRLRR) — A high energy dance routine made famous by the entertainer Soupy Sales. The dancer slides to the left by picking up their left knee and sliding on their right foot. Then, they slide to the right by picking up their R knee and sliding on their L foot. A common pattern is, once to the left, once to the right, and then two slides to the left. Follow this with one right, one left, and two slides to the right. The entire routine generally has the dancer facing square to the audience.

367. SPIN (PIROUETTE) — A turn that is accomplished in one place with one foot planted squarely on the stage.

368. SPIN GIRLS OUT IN PEEL — A line of dance couples are standing either in ballroom dance position or in a pose where the male dancer is holding the female in a hug from behind (or any similar variation of this). The female then spins away from the male with his help in guiding and propelling her. The "peel" suggests that the line of couples performs this turnout one couple right after the other to give it a rippling effect like dominos.

369. SPIN L — Pirouette to the left.

SPIN R — Pirouette to the right.

370. "SPINNERS" PUSHES — A routine made famous by performing groups such as The Spinners or The Temptations in which the dancers hold both fists at 90 degree angles at their sides. Then they step left and bring their feet together as they push those fists in that direction. A common pattern would include 2 pushes left, two pushes right, and then one a piece four more times.

"SPINNERS" PUSHES

371. SPIRIT OF '76 MARCH — A march pattern in which the dancer uses one stiff leg with a very flat foot and the other stepping only on the ball of the foot, so there is a natural up/down look to the march. It is supposed to resemble a soldier who is wounded and has one leg in a cast, unable to bend it. The "Spirit of '76" is a famous painting of three Revolutionary war soldiers marching along with a flag, a fife and a drum. This march helps to capture that spirit.

SPIRIT OF '76 MARCH

372. SQUARE DANCE — A dance for four couples who stand so they form a hollowed out square. It is generally considered country and/or western in style.

SQUISH A BUG: see *307. Push Steps -Squish a Bug*

373. STAGE L — This is the area of the stage that is to the left of the performer as that performer faces the audience. It can also refer to a direction as in "moving stage L" which would suggest that the dancer is moving toward their left if they were facing the audience. If they were facing away from the audience, stage left would actually be to the dancer's right.

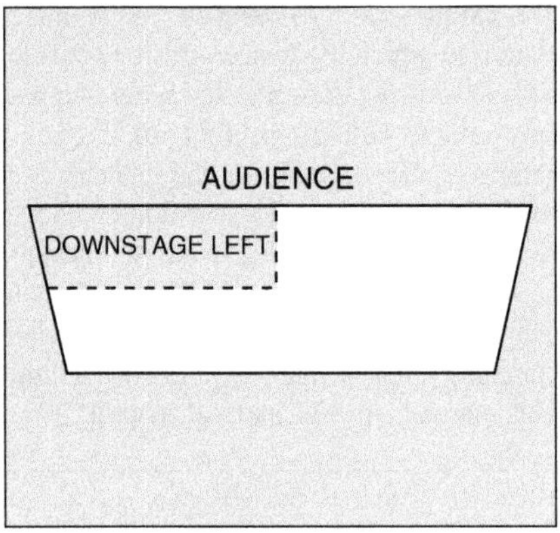

DOWNSTAGE LEFT

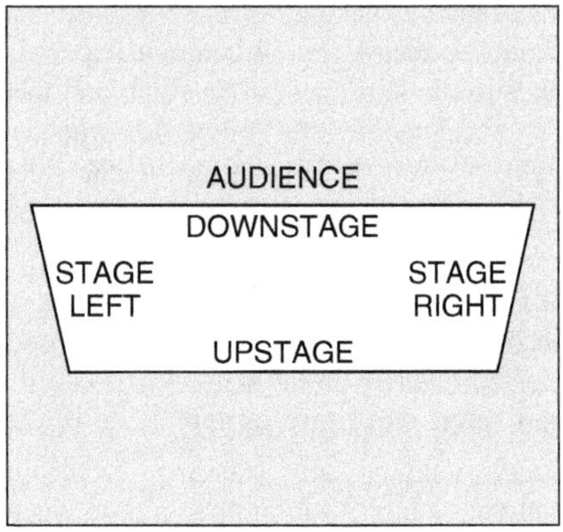

AREAS OF THE STAGE

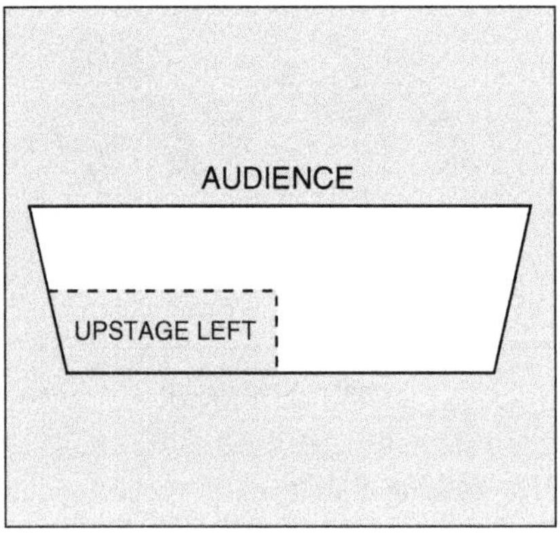

UPSTAGE LEFT

374. STAGE R — This is the area of the stage that is to the right of the performer as that performer faces the audience. It can also refer to a direction as in "moving stage R" which would suggest that the dancer is moving toward their right if they were facing the audience. If they were facing away from the audience, stage right would actually be to the dancer's left.

375. STAND IN A MADRIGAL FASHION WITH LADY'S HAND ON TOP OF MAN'S — An elegant way to stand, reminiscent of old fashioned madrigal groups. The lady places one of her hands on top of the man's outstretched hand as they both face the same direction. They are using opposite hands.

STAND IN A MADRIGAL FASHION WITH LADY'S HAND ON TOP OF MAN'S

376. STAND IN COUPLES ala "AMERICAN GOTHIC" — A pose that is borrowed from the famous Grant painting entitled, "American Gothic." In this painting, as in this pose, the couple is standing side by side, perhaps linking arms. With her free hand, the woman can pretend to hold a basket as the man holds the handle of a pitchfork.

STAND IN COUPLES ala "AMERICAN GOTHIC"

377. STARBURST — A group of dancers standing in a clump or in rows each presents their jazz hands to the audience with arms outstretched from the center of the group. The front rows obviously must be low, the back rows high and the side rows out to their respective sides. The result is a group pose that appears to have rays of light emanating from the center of the group.

STARBURST

378. STEP CLAP — Step to one side followed by a clap usually to that same side. For instance, step left on beat 1 and clap either on the offbeat or on beat 2 also to the left. Repeat to the other side.

379. STEP FLICK KICK — Step onto one foot as if you are running in that direction. Then hop to the other foot in a complete reversal of direction while at the same time kicking back the heel of the foot you originally stepped on. For example, step R facing R on beat 1. Then on 2, hop to the L foot facing L and simultaneously kick the R heel up and back to the R.

380. STEP KICK (SL KR, ETC. OR L KR R KL, ETC.) — Step on one foot followed by a kick of the other foot. The abbreviations indicate which foot you are stepping onto and which one you are kicking. S=step, K=kick, L=left, R=right.

381. STEP KICK FACING FRONT WITH ALTERNATING JAZZ HANDS — As you face the audience, step on your left foot followed by a kick with your right foot. As you kick your right foot, extend your left jazz hand forward at about chest level with palm away from your body. Then, step right and follow that with a kick of your left foot while extending your right jazz hand forward at about chest level.

382. STEP KICK OUT TO THE SIDE (COUNTRY-STYLE) — Facing the audience, step on one foot and then kick the other foot out to its side with a flexed foot.

STEP KICK: see also *76. Country Step Kicks Out to the Side, Flexed Feet* and *260. Partners in Dance Position Step Kick Through Each Other's Legs*

383. STEP SCUFF — Step on one foot and follow that with a scuff of the opposite heel off the floor in front of the "stepping" foot. It's as if you are saying "awe shucks!" Repeat to the other side. This works for soft shoe or easy swing-type dance routines.

384. STEP SLAP THIGHS — With an ongoing step touch pattern (step/together, step/together), slap the sides of your legs as you bring your feet together after the initial step. The pattern becomes step, slap, step, slap.

385. STEP SNAP LOW — Step touching from side to side, snap both fingers on the "touch", moving the hands slightly toward the ground on each snap. You will probably be slightly stooped forward as you perform this routine giving it a low-down-funky-feel.

386. STEP STOMP (TOUCH) OR STEP DIG — This is a four-count pattern beginning with a step on one foot, followed by a stomp of the other foot in front of that initial step. Then step on that stomping foot and stomp the other foot in front of it on beat 4. There is actually no weight put on the stomp, which is why it is called a dig and can be stepped on on the very next beat.

387. STEP TOUCH — Step with one foot followed by a touch of the other foot on the ground next to the first step. Another way to describe this is sometimes "step-together."

STEP TOUCH: see also *137. Funky Step Touches Behind, 138. Funky Step Touches-Heel in Front* and *140. Gospel Style Step Touch*

388. STEP TOUCH AT AN ANGLE WITH "DOO WOP" STYLE SNAPS — With the feet step touching (R first this time) and the body facing slightly downstage L, swing the right hand up so that it snaps overhead on the touch left. Then as you step touch left moving slightly upstage left, swing that same R hand down and snap across the front of your waist. This is reflective of a basic "Doo Wop" song and dance group.

STEP TOUCH AT AN ANGLE WITH "DOO WOP" STYLE SNAPS

389. STOP MARCH — As if you were going to begin marching, lift your left knee up and bring it down so that it reaches the floor on beat 1. Freeze at that moment of contact, so that you basically just stomped the foot on the floor next to the other foot. The arms will move similarly in that they wind up as if to begin a march and then come to a stiff standstill at your sides on the stomp.

390. STOP MARCH FOUR-POINT PIVOT — Perform one STOP MARCH (see above) facing each of the four walls, moving a quarter turn in the same direction after each march.

391. STRADDLE LIFT AROUND MAN'S WAIST — Facing your partner, the female dancer clasps her hands behind the neck of her partner. He holds onto her back at about waist level as she jumps up to sit with one leg on each side of his waist. Her legs are usually straight and either flexed or pointed depending on the style of the dance.

392. STRAIGHT LEG HOPS SWINGING LEGS FROM SIDE TO SIDE (LLRRLLRL) — With very stiff and straight legs swinging from side to side, the dancer hops on the left foot two times, then the right foot two times, left again two times, then once right and once left. The legs are swinging from the waist and resemble a bell swinging from side to side. Notice pattern: 2,2,2,1,1.

STRAIGHT LEG HOPS SWINGING LEGS FROM SIDE TO SIDE (LLRRLLRL)

393. "STREET-WISE" WALK — This basically suggests that the dancer strut with attitude. One way to achieve this is to use the opposite hand of the foot you are stepping onto to scoop down and in front of yourself at about waist level as you step.

STROLL: see *262. Partners Stroll Arm in Arm* and *415. The Stroll*

394. SUGAR FOOT — Standing with your feet apart and on the balls of both feet, twist back and forth with each step that you take. The toes of both feet are facing in the same direction on each step as if you are squashing something under your feet. This is a 1940s move appropriate to the Jitterbug and Lindy.

395. SURF POSE — The dancer stands with feet apart, one foot somewhat more downstage than the other. They should crouch slightly with their hands out, palms down as if they are balancing and actually surfing.

SURF POSE

396. SURF ROCK — In a SURF POSE (see above), the dancer shifts their entire weight forward and back without ever actually moving their feet.

SURRENDER: see *162. Hands Up ala Surrender*

397. SWAY — Rock your entire body from side to side either from a standing, sitting or kneeling position. Usually the sway is performed by leading with the shoulder in the direction you are moving.

398. SWAY SNAP — A step touch in which both hands swing the direction you are stepping and then snap on that side as you touch together. Everything is moving in the same direction.

399. SWAY SNAP (step/touch) PLAYING IMAGINARY GUITARS — The same as a SWAY SNAP in that everything is moving the same direction in this step together. The only difference is that the arms are held in such a way as though you are pretending to play a guitar as you step touch.

400. SWIM — Standing with feet apart or together and one knee slightly bent so you can "bop" on the beat, move your arms as though you are swimming. The Backstroke, Breaststroke, American Crawl and any others are all acceptable. This is a 1950s and 1960s dance born out of the beach music and movies of that era.

401. SWING HIPS — Bend your knees slightly so you can isolate your hips and swing them from side to side.

SWING HIPS: see also *109. Feet Apart Swing Hips-Pooh Hips*

402. SWING OPERA HANDS SIDE TO SIDE — Clasp your hands with one on top of the other, fingertips of one hand meet the inside knuckles of the other. This is a caricature of an opera recitalist. Swing those clasped hands to and fro at chest level.

403. SWING R LEG R L R L — Like Ray Bolger (the scarecrow in the movie, The Wizard of Oz,) hop on your left foot as you swing your right leg forward, back, forward and back. On the second "back," put the right leg down so that you can hop on it and swing the left leg forward, back, forward, back.

SWING R LEG R L R L

404. SWING YOUR PARTNERS — Taken from square dancing routines, face your partner and link same elbows (i.e. R) so that your (R) shoulders are together. Run, walk or skip around each other, held together by your own elbows. Reverse and link L elbows and circle the opposite direction.

SWING YOUR PARTNERS

405. SWINGING A LASSO — Put one hand overhead and swing it around and around as if you were a cowboy swinging a rope.

406. SWIVEL BOTH KNEES — With your feet and legs held tightly together, bend your knees and make one complete revolution as they both move in the same direction. Try moving them down to the right, down center, down to the left and back to standing up straight in one fluid motion.

SWOON: see *158. Hand to Forehead ala Swoon*

T

407. TANGO — A ballroom dance of Latin American origin in 4/4 time with a basic pattern of step-step-step, step close, and characterized by long poses and stylized body positions. A basic routine is to stand as couples in ballroom dance position and walk three steps in one direction with the held hands very straight in the arms. Then reverse hands and direction for three more steps in the other direction.

TANGO

TANGO: see also *257. Partner-less Tango*

408. TAP TRIPLETS R L R L R L — An athletic tap dance routine in which the dancer does a shuffle with the right foot out to the right followed by a shuffle with the left foot out to the left. Repeat this routine over and over achieving a "1 and a 2 and a 3 and a 4 and a" triplet pattern.

409. TEMPTATIONS PUSHES — Interchangeable with the "Spinners" move. A routine made famous by performing groups such as The Spinners or The Temptations in which the dancers hold both fists at 90 degree angles at their sides. They then step left and bring their feet together as they push those fists in that direction. A common pattern would include 2 pushes left, two pushes right, and then one a piece four more times.

410. TEXAS STAR — A group of dancers, (usually at least four as in a square dance,) all face one direction around a circle holding onto each other as couples. The inside person of each couple puts their free hand into the center of the circle of couples so that the group begins to resemble a wheel with those extended arms resembling the spokes. Then, the couples walk around in the circle the direction they are facing. Sometimes this is called a "PINWHEEL."

TEXAS STAR

411. THE ALLIGATOR — (1) The dancers lie flat on their backs with feet and arms wiggling in the air like an alligator who has somehow found himself flat on his back and is floundering. (2) With arms outstretched in front of you, the dancer opens and closes their arms like the jaws of a big alligator. This second definition is sometimes called "The Crocodile Smile."

THE ALLIGATOR

412. THE FREDDY — A dance that bears a striking resemblance to a Jumping Jack exercise. The dancer begins with feet together and hands at your sides. Keeping all of the weight on one foot, swing both straight arms and one leg out to your sides as high as they can go and then back again to the sides. Next, do the same using the other leg.

THE FREDDY

413. THE JERK — On beat 1, reach one hand over your head and the other somewhat behind your back while at the same time thrusting your chest and ribcage out in front of you to the side of the higher hand. On beat 2, throw both hands forward and violently bring the chest and ribcage to a contracted position.

T

THE JERK

THIGH LIFT GIRL'S FEET TOWARD THE CEILING

414. THE SMURF — This consists of a four-count grapevine step that ends with a hitching up of the knee as opposed to a touch. For example, if you are beginning the step moving to the left with your shoulders square to the audience, you would step first onto your left foot, cross behind or in front with the right on 2, again to the left on 3 and then hitch up your right knee to about waist high on 4. Repeat to the other side.

415. THE STROLL — An eight-count grapevine step, or series of steps that was a popular group dance in the 1950s and 1960s. In this dance the grapevine is often executed while facing a partner and moving through two parallel lines of dancers that are forming a lane in the middle of the dance floor.

416. THIGH LIFT GIRL'S FEET TOWARD THE CEILING — From a ballroom dance position, the male dancer swings the female so that both of her legs pass on one side of him and continue toward the ceiling. She comes to rest with the small of her back resting on his thigh with her feet still toward the ceiling.

417. THREE-COUNT SALUTE — A stagy salute in which beat 1 has the dancer bringing their right hand to their forehead while at the same time bending both knees slightly. On beat 2 the legs straighten up and the right hand goes straight up overhead with fingers still tightly together and outstretched. On beat 3 the arm and hand come back to their side.

418. THREE-PERSON SHOULDER LIFT — All facing the same direction, two dancers are lifting another so that the lifted dancer comes to rest sitting on the lifters' shoulders. A variation would have the lifted dancer actually standing between the two lifters as they support with their arms.

THREE-PERSON SHOULDER LIFT

419. THREE-POINT TURN — Also referred to as a Chaîne turn (see page 13), it involves one complete revolution that takes 3 steps to accomplish while the dancer continues to move in the direction they are turning. For example, as they use three steps to turn to their left, they are also moving further toward stage left. There is no turn on step 1 (L). On 2 (R) the dancer should be halfway around and facing upstage. On 3 (L) the dancer is again facing front.

420. THUMBS IN BELT, ROCK L AND R WITH BOWED LEGS — Standing with your feet in second position (apart), bend your legs slightly and shift the weight of your entire body from left to right, back and forth. With your thumbs hooked into your real or imaginary belt loops, or the waistband of your trousers, you will give off a distinctly western flair.

421. THUMBS TO CHEST — Indicating "me" or "I," simply point your thumbs toward yourself with elbows slightly raised. Turn your body slightly to the side to give a more stylized effort.

422. THUMBS TO SELF (Same as "thumbs to chest") — Indicating "me" or "I," simply point your thumbs toward yourself with elbows slightly raised. Turn your body slightly to the side to give a more stylized effort.

423. TIME STEP (DOUBLE, TRIPLE, SINGLE) — Perhaps the most common and basic tap routines, the TIME STEP is a staple of a tap dancer's vocabulary. Each TIME STEP takes exactly four counts and amounts to a series of stomps, shuffles, flaps and steps. The "Single," "Double" and "Triple" refer to the number of shuffles used within the four counts.

424. TOE (FLAP) HEEL BACK STEP — A basic tap dance or soft shoe step in which the dancer steps or (flaps) their foot out to the side on counts 1-2 (L) followed by a backstep 3-4 (RL).

TOE: see also 9. *Alternating Toe Touchers*

425. TRAIN ARMS — With 90 degree bent elbows, churn them by your sides like the wheels of an old fashioned railroad train.

TRAIN ARMS

426. TRAIN STEP — (1) Step forward with your left foot, (2) back with your right, (3) further back with your left, and (4) forward with your right. In actuality, the right foot is stepping in the same place both times but because of the forward and backward nature of the left foot, it seems that the right is moving back and forth, too. The feet movement looks like a train wheel cranking along.

427. TRAIN STEP FOUR-POINT PIVOT — Performing one TRAIN STEP (four steps, see above) toward each wall for a total of 16 steps. The same foot is leading on each step and you keep turning the same direction on each quarter turn. Add the train arms or another variation if you so choose.

428. TRAVEL ARMS L R — Churning your fists around each other in a rapid fashion, just like a basketball referee does when he calls a "traveling violation," two counts left and then two counts right in a 4/4 measure. This hand move has a distinctive Latin feel, but can also work in Rock and Roll, and other places.

429. TRAVEL ARMS LOW TO HIGH — Churning your fists around each other like a referee does in basketball when he calls a "traveling violation," move the churning fists from low in front of you up toward the ceiling.

430. TRAVEL ARMS WITH STYLIZED "PONY" — Churning your fists around each other like a referee does in basketball when he calls a "traveling violation," move your feet in the three-step pattern of the PONY. The PONY consists of a step followed by a ball change, repeated over and over.

431. TRENCHES OPPOSITE ARM LEG — Trenches involve running with very straight legs, leaning forward and swinging your straight arms. In this instance the arms are swung in opposition so that when you are stepping on your left leg, your right arm is forward.

TRENCHES OPPOSITE ARM LEG

432. TRENCHES SAME ARM LEG — Trenches involve running with very straight legs, leaning forward and swinging your straight arms. In this instance the arms are swung in unison with the leg so that when you are stepping on your left leg, your left arm is forward.

TRENCHES SAME ARM LEG

433. TRUCKIN' — With the index finger of one hand held in the air, the dancer step-hops either in place or moving. The dancer leads slightly with their chest in the direction of the step-hop, then repeats to the other side. This step is used often in dances of the 1930s to 1950s.

TRUCKIN'

434. TURN JAZZ HANDS IN AND BRING FINGERS TOGETHER OVERHEAD — With spread fingers, rotate the hands from the wrist and elbow and bring the hands together so they go to "pray" hands overhead. The pose will be distinctly Eastern.

TURN: see also *194. Inside Turn, 252. Outside Turn* and *419. Three-Point Turn*

435. TWIST — A dance made famous by Chubby Checker in which the dancer simply rises to the balls of their feet and twists their lower body in opposition to their upper body over and over again.

TWIST: see also *99. Eight-Count Twist* and *363. Slow Twist Lean LR*

436. TWIST FOOT TOE HEEL TOE HEEL — Hopping on one foot (i.e. left) the dancer alternates touching the other foot to the floor, first the toe then the heel and back and forth. This would be done off to the same side as the foot, which in this case is the right.

437. TWO-POINT PIVOT — Four marching steps that allow the dancer to do a complete turn around and end up at the same place they started. (1) Step straight ahead L, (2) pivot 180 degrees to the right and step toward the back wall R, (3) step toward the back wall with the L foot, (4) pivot 180 degrees to the right and step toward the front with the R foot, so that you are back to where you began.

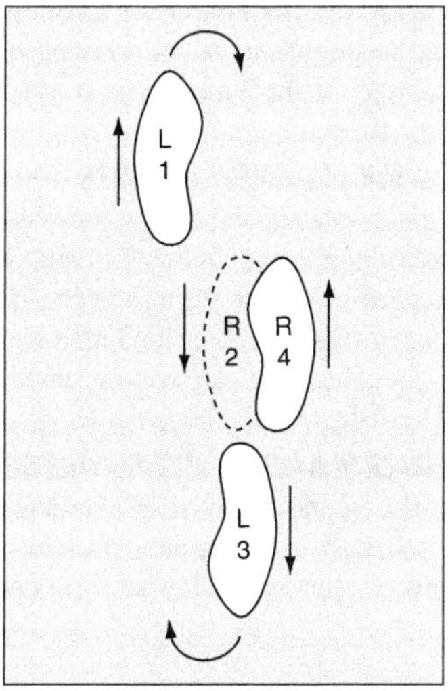

TWO-POINT PIVOT

438. TWO-POINT PIVOT BURST — Perform a four count two-point pivot (see above). On the first step add to this a burst of the arms from high to low in one count.

439. TWO-POINT PIVOT WITH CLAPS — Perform a four count two-point pivot (see above). Clap your hands on beats 2 and 4.

U

440. U-DIP — With your feet apart, plié deeply (bend your knees) and then straighten them up so that you are putting your weight on the left foot and are facing stage right. Repeat to the other side by again bending your knees and then straightening them so that the weight goes to the right foot and you face stage left. The motion of bending and straightening causes the dancer to make a "U" with their entire body, thus the name of the step. Notice the feet never lose contact with the ground and are in the same place throughout the U-DIP. There are no "steps" involved, only weight changes and body angles.

441. U-DIPS AWAY FROM PARTNER — Partners are standing side by side and each perform a U-DIP (see above). At the end they are essentially facing one another.

U-DIPS AWAY FROM PARTNER

U-DIP: see also *80. Couples U-Dip Holding Front to Back*

442. U-DIP L R — Perform U-DIPS to the left and then to the right. When a direction is indicated, it is the direction the body is moving, which is opposite to where the dancer will end up facing when they finish that particular step. In other words, a U-DIP L will end with the dancer actually facing stage right.

443. U-DIPS DRAWING GUNS — Perform U-DIPS (see above), and as you bend your knees slap the sides of your legs. As you straighten the legs to face one side, pretend to draw pistols from holsters. Point the index finger and thumb like the barrel and hammer of a pistol.

444. U-STEPS — Keeping your body square to the audience, perform a step touch pattern (step together). As you step, bend your knees and as you bring your feet together, straighten your legs so that the body has made a "U" in the air. Notice that the difference between this step and a U-DIP is that on a U-STEP the dancer is actually moving their feet. It truly is a U STEP. Also there is no turning of the body angle.

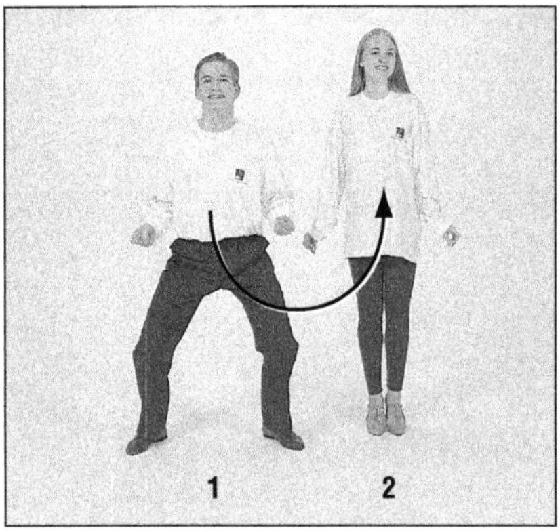

U-STEPS

445. UPSTAGE — This is the area of the stage furthest away from the audience. To move UPSTAGE is to move away from the audience. On a raked stage (one built with an incline away from the audience), the performer actually has to move uphill to move UPSTAGE.

V

446. VAUDEVILLE ROCK — With jazz hands held at about shoulder level and facing toward the audience, the dancer rocks the entire body, especially the hands and hips, left and right with a lot of energy. A variation would be to raise the jazz hands so they were actually waving overhead as the body rocked left and right.

VAUDEVILLE ROCK

W

447. not on video

447. WAG R INDEX FINGER AT AUDIENCE — In time to the music, simply accent your R index finger at the audience as if you were scolding them.

448. WALK ala JIMMY DURANTE — This is a character walk made famous by the legendary performer, Jimmy Durante. It is a stiff-legged walk with the upstage hand open by your upstage cheek or holding a hat. The short chugging steps are accompanied by a rapid headshake and a huge smile.

449. WALK IN A CIRCLE AROUND YOURSELF — In as many counts as the music allows (usually 4, 6, or 8), walk in a circle around an imaginary pole and end up right back where you started.

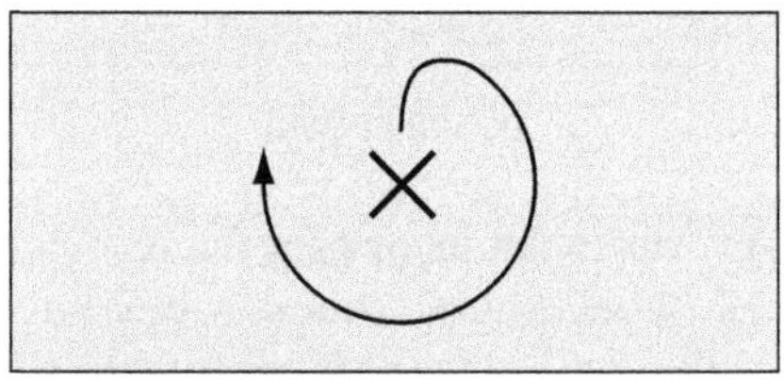

WALK IN CIRCLE AROUND YOURSELF

450. not on video

450. WALK IN CIRCLE AROUND SELF AWAY FROM PARTNER — Couples standing next to each other and facing the audience each make a simultaneous CIRCLE AROUND YOURSELF (see above) in opposite directions ending up side by side again right where they started. At 1/4 of the way around they are the furthest apart from each other.

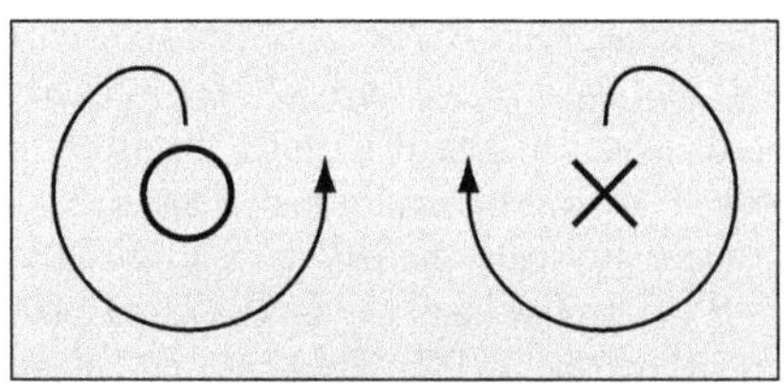

WALK IN CIRCLE AROUND SELF
AWAY FROM PARTNER

451. WALK IN COUNTRY STYLE — Walk either in place or moving somewhere. Keep your knees turned out and perhaps bow-legged with your feet flexed to give the walk a "country" feel. Your hands could slap your thighs on beats 2 and 4, hook in your belt loops, swish your skirt, or assume any other variety of "countrified" moves.

452. WALK IN PLACE — Move your feet in time with the music as if you were walking but don't go anywhere.

453. WALK STAGE L — Move your feet in time with the music and travel to the performer's L as they face the audience.

454. WALK STAGE R — Move your feet in time with the music and travel to the performer's R as they face the audience.

455. WALKING KNEE POPS — With your feet together, alternate bending one knee and then the other so they pop out in front of you. It is as if you were walking without even picking up your feet. This can look either funky, Latin, smooth or many other ways depending on the tempo and style in which you walk.

WALKING KNEE POPS

456. WALTZ — A very old and popular dance done in a count of three (3/4 time). The basic WALTZ simply involves a step forward followed by two steps in place, then a step back followed by two more steps in place. It can be performed in a stationary place or spinning around the room. Still the basic pattern will always be to step on 1 accenting that beat, followed by light steps on 2 and 3.

WALTZ: see also *82. Couples Waltz in Circles Around the Stage* and *166. Hesitation Waltz*

457. WALTZ IN DANCE POSITION — Using that three-step pattern of the basic WALTZ (see above), dancers perform as couples in ballroom dance position for an elegant and timeless dance.

458. WATUSI — With 90 degree bent elbows, right over left in front of you, alternate them up and down with the fist of one hand above the elbow of the other.

459. WAVE R HAND LRLR — With the hand overhead, bend it at the elbow as it moves as big as is possible from left to right, back and forth. Perform with a lot of energy so the body moves as well.

460. WAVE, TURN PALM UP ON CUTOFF — With a jazz hand shimmying overhead, stop moving it as it turns in toward your body for a final cutoff that leaves you standing like the Statue of Liberty.

WAVE: see also *33. Both Hands Wave Overhead*

WHACK: see *232. Major Whack Attack* and *243. Minor Whack Attack*

461. WIGGLE LEGS — With your feet apart and knees slightly bent, bring them together and apart in an undulating fashion.

462. WIND UP TO PRESENT HIGH — Begin with both hands to one side of your slightly twisted body. It is as if you are about to throw a discus. Swing both arms so that they go overhead to a JAZZ HAND PRESENT. You will end up looking like the letter "Y."

463. WINDMILL ARMS — Beginning with both arms on one side of your body, swing them overhead in a big arch so they end up on the other side of yourself. If you are swinging them from right to left, the left hand will be leading slightly or vice versa.

464. WINDMILL ARMS IN RIPPLE — Perform the WINDMILL ARMS as described above. This can be very effective if performed by an entire group in a rippling, domino-like fashion from one side of the stage to the other, like a stadium wave.

465. WINDMILL ARMS TURN L R — This is a more specific direction that would tell the performer which way the WINDMILL ARMS (see above) should be executed. In this case it is from stage right to left leading with the left arm, the right trailing slightly behind in its arch.

466. WIPE — Slice both hands in front of your waist with palms down like the move an umpire makes when calling a runner "safe" in baseball. It gives off a message of *no, nothing, not, never* or other such words. This could also be accompanied by more specific directions that might send a different message such as wipe overhead, *wipe one hand, or wipe with hands at a diagonal.*

WIPE

467. WIPE BOTH HANDS LIKE "SAFE" IN BASEBALL — (see WIPE above).

468. WIPE BROW — With one hand, pretend to wipe the sweat from your brow, indicating heat or exhaustion to the audience.

469. not on video

469. WIPE OPEN PALM ACROSS EYES — With your palm turned out toward the audience, move your hand in front of your eyes without actually touching your face. This will send a message of *seeing, eyes, vision, look!*, etc.

470. WIPE SCISSORS HANDS — Like the movement of a large scissors, the dancer moves their hands and arms back and forth, one over the other. In this case the accent is usually put where the hands are crossed as opposed to when they are open.

471. WOMEN SIT ON MEN'S KNEE — With the male dancer kneeling on one knee, his female partner sits on his other knee or thigh. He should make certain that the knee she is sitting on is well supported by his foot and lower leg. If need be, the female should be able to support some of her own weight as well.

WOMEN SIT ON MEN'S KNEE

472. WORM ARMS — Waving your arms alternating from side to side, always leading with your elbow and then "developing" the lower arm and hand so that the arms almost slither like a snake or worm. When standing upright, the arms should be held slightly back like the wings of a large bird.

473. WRAPS (HIGH) — With both arms moving simultaneously from one side to the other, they begin by being wrapped around your waist, the right arm in front and the left behind. They then reach high above your head in as big an arch as possible until they get to the other side and end up with the left arm wrapped across the front of the waist and the right arm behind.

474. WRAPS (LOW) — With both arms moving simultaneously from one side to the other, they begin by being wrapped around your waist, the right arm in front and the left behind. They then reach way out in front of you toward the audience at about waist or chest level, in as big an arch as possible. When they get to the other side, they end up with the left arm wrapped across the front of the waist and the right arm behind.

Y

475. not on video

475. YELLOW BRICK ROAD STEP — This is a dance step that was made famous in the movie "The Wizard of Oz" as the main characters were traveling down the Yellow Brick Road. Step onto your left heel on beat 1. On 2, step with your right foot behind the left. On the "and" of 2 quickly step onto the ball of the left foot and then reverse those two and a half counts beginning on the heel of the right foot. This step can be performed in one place or used to travel from one point to the next.

ACKNOWLEDGEMENTS

My very special thanks to

Linda Rann: For coordinating the photos and video production, and for being a good friend.

Michael O'Hearn: For assisting with the location shoot.

Shelley Kaler: Photographer

The wonderful student models, John Avant, Melissa Lescota, Ryan Perkins, and Kim McDowel from Newman Smith High School in Carrollton, Texas under the direction of Elizabeth Volk.

John, Melissa, Ryan, Kim

Students like these make it fun to be a teacher!